WTO

Regulation of World Trade after the Uruguay Round

Richard Senti

Center for Economic Research, Swiss Federal Institute of Technology Zurich, Switzerland

Patricia Conlan

Law Department, University of Limerick, Ireland

Schulthess Polygraphischer Verlag 1998

Foreword

The World Trade Organization marked its first two years of existence with the Ministerial Conference in Singapore in December 1996. There, trade ministers from more than 130 WTO Member countries applauded the achievements of the new organization and the set of multilateral trade rules it represents. Indeed, the achievements of the WTO during its first two years of operation have been astounding. However, this would never have been possible had the WTO not been able to draw from the experiences of the GATT, the multilateral agreement which contributed so much to liberalizing global trade throughout its 47-year history.

Even with the benefits of the Uruguay Round and the recent push to liberalize trade in telecommunications, financial services and in information technology products, trade liberalization is incomplete in many key areas.

Trade flows have multiplied fifteen-fold in the last four decades - reaching $6,000 billion last year while production has increased six-fold. The worldwide movement of foreign direct investment is even more striking. In the ten years to 1996, investment flows worldwide easily quadrupled, from around $60 billion to almost $300 billion per annum. Unprecedented growth rates of certain industrializing countries in Asia and Latin America are evidence that a huge shift in economic power is underway.

The world needs a strong WTO simply because the WTO reflects and represents the global economy as it really is. It is more in tune with economic reality and practical business than any other similar economic institution or legal framework. But it cannot stand still, it must go on developing and keeping pace with events and change.

Renato Ruggiero
Geneva, November 1997

Contents

3

Contents

Contents

Abbreviations

BBl	Bundesblatt (Switzerland)
BISD	Basic Instruments and Selected Documents (GATT)
CCC	Customs Co-operation Council
CIS	Commonwealth of Independent States
Cttee	Committee
DSB	Dispute Settlement Body
EC	European Communities, European Community
EEC	European Economic Community
EU	European Union
FAO	Food and Agriculture Organization
GATS	General Agreement on Trade in Services
GATT	General Agreement on Tariffs and Trade
ITO	International Trade Organization
LDC	Least-Developed Countries
MFA	Multifibre Agreement
MFN	Most-Favoured-Nation clause
MTN	Multilateral Trade Negotiations
NTBs	Non-Tariff Barriers
NZZ	Neue Zürcher Zeitung
SDR	Special Drawing Rights, 1 SDR = ca 1.38 US$
SPM	Sanitary and Phytosanitary Measures
SR	Systematische Sammlung des schweizerischen Bundesrechts
TMB	Textiles Monitoring Body
TRIMS	Trade-Related Investment Measures
TRIPS	Trade-Related Aspects of Intellectual Property Rights
UNCTAD	United Nations Conference on Trade and Development
UN	United Nations
WIPO	World Intellectual Property Organization
WTO	World Trade Organization

Introduction

The conclusion of the Uruguay Round in Geneva on 15 December 1993 followed by the signing of the Agreements in Marrakesh on 15 April 1994 meant both a continuation and an expansion of the General Agreement on Tariffs and Trade (GATT). A continuation in that the newly created world trading system took over the ground rules of the GATT, and an expansion in that this new system now extends beyond trade in goods to include trade in services and the protection of intellectual property rights. The Agreements entered into force on 1 January 1995.

The new world trading system rests on three pillars. The first pillar is the existing GATT, extended by twelve Agreements on agriculture, textiles, dumping, subsidies, etc. The Agreement on Trade in Services comprises the second pillar and the third pillar is made up of the Agreement on the Protection of Intellectual Property Rights. In addition to these Agreements, which are binding on all WTO Members, there are Agreements on the International Trade in Civil Aircraft and Government Procurement. These two Agreements are binding only on the ratifying states. Two additional Agreements - on Dairy and Bovine Meat Products - will be terminated at the end of 1997. The institutional element required by the Agreements is provided by the World Trade Organization, situated in Geneva.

The aim of this book is to sketch for the reader how the individual Agreements came about, what their scope is and how they function institutionally. The book should act as a tool in accessing the new world trading system and in understanding the translation of the international Agreements into national law.

The material for this book stems largely from a publication - in German, in 1994 - *GATT-WTO. Die neue Welthandelsordnung nach der Uruguay-Runde* by *Richard Senti*, updated to include the first WTO Ministerial Conference held on 9 - 12 December 1996 in Singapore and the additional negotiations in 1997 about trade in services. Additional contributions were made by Patricia Conlan, who also did the translation.

Although the term European Union (EU) is now in common usage, the term European Communities (EC) is used here. This reflects the fact that the European Communities enjoy legal personality (not the European Union) and the European Communities are WTO Members (not the European Union).

Special thanks are due to Markus König, lic. oec. publ., Center for Economic Research, ETH, Zurich, for checking the first draft of this publication, to Susanne Böhm Frei for her help with the manuscript and to Fiona Mc Goldrick, B.A., Dip. In LIB (NUI) for compiling the index.

November 1997

Richard Senti, Zurich

Patricia Conlan, Limerick

1. The Establishment of the World Trade Organization

The conclusion of the Uruguay Round in Geneva on 15 December 1993, followed by the signing of the Agreements in Marrakesh four months later, marked the beginning of a new world trading system. This new system is the continuation of the General Agreement on Tariffs and Trade (GATT), widened and deepened as a result of the 1986-1993 Uruguay Round negotiations.

1.1 Starting Point

The creation of the GATT in the wake of the Second World War was due in large part to American initiatives. The USA had two objectives at that time: given the chaotic circumstances of the post-war period the Americans saw themselves increasingly as responsible for the establishment of democracy and for the liberal economic order. It was envisaged that the new world trading system would guarantee open foreign markets as well as market economies and matching structures in trading partner countries. This in turn would both underpin the American idea of freedom and help to give it even more prominence. There was an additional factor in that the American economy had to be transformed after 1945 from a war economy to a peacetime economy, and the returning servicemen reintegrated into economic activity. The USA therefore had a policy of open foreign markets. The American vision of the anticipated world trading system was a deliberate extension of the New Deal of the 1930s and of the 1934 Trade Act. This statute contained the most important principles of the new world trading system.

It would be useful to examine the economic background against which the American proposals for the restructuring of the world trading system were made.

In order to tackle the recession of the 1930s the Americans had drafted the Smoot-Hawley Tariff Act which provided for an increase in tariffs from an average of 26 to around 50 percent. The proposal encountered enormous resistance from all sectors of the economy. Despite this, the President, *Herbert Hoover*, signed the new foreign trade act into law in

1930. America's trading partners responded to the US high tariff policy with corresponding counter measures. The result of this trade war was a reduction of over 30 percent in international trade.

1932 saw the Democrats' candidate, *Franklin D. Roosevelt*, successfully challenge President *Herbert Hoover*, who had been nominated for re-election by the Republican Party. The victory for the Democrats was clearly as a result of the promise to steer the American economy out of the increasingly difficult economic crisis. Two years after taking up office *Franklin D. Roosevelt* signed a new trade act. In form it was an extension of the Smoot-Hawley Tariff Act but in substance it represented a new approach by the US to foreign trade. This act is known in the literature as the "Hull Program", because of its author, Secretary of State *Cordell Hull*. It is also known as the "Reciprocal Trade Agreements Act (1934)" - obviously because of the contents.

The 1934 act had three objectives: elimination of trade barriers; non-discrimination between trading partners (principle of Most-Favoured-Nation, MFN); reciprocity in negotiations. All three objectives are to be found in GATT and consequently in the current world trading system.

- Elimination of trade barriers: *Cordell Hull* wanted to eliminate all trade barriers - internally and externally - in order to promote American export trade. *Cordell Hull* told Congress that the main thrust of this proposal was the reopening of former outlets and the opening up of new opportunities for American overcapacity. In order to facilitate achieving these objectives, the act gave the President the power to conclude treaties covering tariff reductions up to 50 percent of the current tariff level. This power was limited in time; however, it has been prolonged a total of eleven times - at intervals of one to four years - and was finally repealed only in 1967.

During the latter half of the 1940s it was a commonly held view among leading Democrats in the US that the failure of an open world trading system in the 1930s lay at the heart of the outbreak of hostilities. The USA was therefore under an obligation, in order to secure world peace and to combat Communism, to promote a free trade system.

- Non-discrimination between trading partners (principle of Most-Fa-voured-Nation - MFN): a second key point of the Hull Program was the principle of Most-Favoured-Nation - MFN. All advantages, favours, privileges, immunities which the US granted to a trading partner were accorded to all parties with which the US had concluded an agreement - immediately and unconditionally. The principle of Most-Favoured-Nation was restricted in 1951 with the exclusion of the Communist states.

Given the operation of the "doctrine of the principal supplier" the application of the principle of Most-Favoured-Nation as it then applied should be seen in relative terms. In order to ensure that their own position was not weakened too much as a result of an extension of the tariff concessions to the other trading partners, the Americans negotiated tariff reductions only with principal suppliers.

- Negotiations in accordance with the principle of reciprocity: a third feature of the US foreign trade legislation of that period was the principle of reciprocity. This was the basis for the term "Reciprocal Trade Agreements Act". The Americans were only committed to an elimination of trade barriers vis-à-vis those trading partners who reciprocated. The demand for reciprocity arose in the context of the improvement of the exchange relationships, employment and the balance of payments - the very same arguments which continue to be made today.

1.2   The Failure of the ITO

In November 1945 the American State Department published the "Proposals for Expansion of World Trade and Employment". In February 1946 the UN Economic and Social Council decided to hold an international conference for trade and employment with the intention of creating an international organization for trade and employment - similar to the emerging Bretton Woods institutions (International Monetary Fund and World Bank). In October of the same year, eighteen of the nineteen countries invited came together in London for a first preparatory conference. The Soviet Union did not take up the invitation, giving as its reason that the time available for preparation was too brief. In reality the (then) USSR was not interested in foreign trade at that time. The working paper of the conference was the "Suggested Charter for an International Trade Organization". The actual contents represented only a slightly varied version of the proposal put forward by the US in the previous Spring.

Following the necessary preparations, the UN Conference on Trade and Employment took place in Havana from November 1947 to March 1948. Some 54 states signed the "Havana Charter for an International Trade Organization" (ITO) on 24 March 1948. The Charter contained provisions on the general objectives of the Organization, on employment, economic development and recovery, trade policy (this section corresponded in a wide measure to the later GATT), international competition, bilateral treaties covering primary products and the creation of an institution to realize and implement the Charter.

The Havana Charter, which was due in large measure to the initiative of the American Executive (State Department), eventually emerged in the American Legislature (Congress) for decision. The majority of the legislators were opposed to the ITO - though for different reasons. Those of a liberal persuasion were opposed to it as they saw the ITO as too protectionist, whereas for the protectionists it was too liberal. The rejection of the Havana Charter in business and political circles led the US President, *Harry S. Truman,* to decide in 1950 not to present the Charter to Congress. The fate of the ITO was sealed when the Charter was not ratified by the Americans.

What caused the collapse of the efforts of the delegates to the negotiations? Why could the Americans not proceed with their Hull Program in a revised format and relieve international trade of the ever-increasing national trade barriers? No doubt there is more than one reason for what happened. Firstly, the strategy of collaboration with the UK was unfortunate. The draft presented by the American delegation as its own proposal contained a number of exceptions put forward by the British, which the Americans, in later negotiations, were no longer prepared to push (balance of payments related exceptions). In addition to this, the British were not prepared to forego their Commonwealth preferences (which a few years later they did). Finally, the exceptions proposed by the sectoral representative bodies (agriculture and transport) impeded a more effective liberalization of trade.

In the course of the negotiations it seemed that each of these grounds had contributed to changing the positive attitude of the Americans, in the first instance to one of scepticism and eventually to one of total exasperation. The American delegate *Clair Wilcox* warned the negotiating partners about ever more far-reaching demands and exceptions, and also warned against the misguided assumption that they could make use of the protectionist provisions, whereas the US had committed itself to the principle of free trade and market access. These signs of disagreement put a question mark over the Havana negotiations once again. It was clear that the American signature to the ITO statutes came with the unarticulated reservation that the Legislature would have the final word in the matter.

1.3   The GATT as a "Temporary Solution"

At the first preparatory conference in 1946 the participating states decided as a preliminary step to regulate the reductions offered by the US in the tariff and non-tariff barriers' area by means of a special agreement outside the ITO. It was intended to incorporate this agreement as Part IV in the ITO as drafted. The sequence came about because the creation of a world-wide trade organization took longer than anticipated. There was also general consensus on the need for the speedy reduction of the trade barriers arising from the wartime period. What was also decisive for an accelerated approach was the fact that the American offer - based on the Trade Act then in force - was due to expire at the end of 1947. It was decided to tackle the matter by means of an agreement rather than by means of an organization because the Trade Act restricted the legal competence of the American Administration to the conclusion of trade treaties. It remained the prerogative of the Legislature to decide whether or not to accede to an organization. As a result of this, great care was taken in drafting the GATT to ensure that only those provisions which corresponded to a trade treaty were taken from the draft ITO statutes.

The first draft of the General Agreement on Tariffs and Trade emerged in Lake Success, New York, in the Spring of 1947. There were further negotiations in Geneva in the Autumn of the same year. The conference participants exchanged their lists of exceptions, while at the same time withholding possible tariff concessions which they were prepared to offer on a reciprocal basis to their fellow negotiating parties. The negotiations proceeded product by product and on a bilateral basis. Although this approach was exceptionally difficult, a successful outcome was helped by the fact that at that time so many countries were dependent on the dollar and access to the dollar market was welcome. This was all the more desirable because of the fact that due to their own balance of payments difficulties they could not remove barriers in advance nor did they have to accept tariff reduction obligations until a later point in time. The one hundred plus decisions which emerged from the negotiations eventually formed the General Agreement on Tariffs and Trade which was signed by 23 states in Geneva on 30 October 1947. The states concerned were: Australia, Belgium, Brazil, Burma, Canada, Ceylon, Chile, China, Cuba, Czechoslovakia, France, India, Lebanon, Luxembourg, Netherlands, New Zealand, Norway, Pakistan, Rhodesia, Syria, Union of South Africa, United Kingdom and United States of America.

The Agreement entered into force on 1 January 1948 for eight states - Australia, Belgium, Canada, France, Luxembourg, Netherlands, United Kingdom and United States of America. The remaining states ratified the Agreement in the following months.

The contracting parties settled on a provisional application of the Agreement. They took the view that when the International Trade Organization was established this would form part of the final structure. However, the ITO was not established and as a result, the legal basis for the world trading system remained in this provisional form of the GATT.

1.4 From the GATT to the WTO

The further development of the world trading system came about in the wake of trade negotiations or trade rounds. The sequence can be seen in Table 1.

To date eight rounds have taken place within the framework of the GATT - some of them named after the initiator, some named after the location where negotiations commenced. In the first three rounds the emphasis was on the accession of new GATT contracting parties and the reduction of tariffs.

The fourth round in 1955 was of considerable importance for the continuation of the GATT in that the contracting parties reaffirmed their acceptance of the Agreement in the current form. The amendments and additions were confined to the relatively unimportant reformulation of the Preamble, the laying down of a procedure for the periodic withdrawal of concessions and the annual examination of payment-related trade restrictions.

The GATT was further widened in 1966 (Kennedy Round) with the inclusion of special and differential treatment exceptions aimed at improving market access for the non-industrial countries vis-à-vis the industrial countries (Part IV Trade and Development).

The focus of the seventh round (Tokyo Round) was primarily the elimination of non-tariff barriers to trade, followed by the new regulation of dumping, subsidies, government procurement and tariff preferences for non-industrial countries.

Arising from these changes the GATT underwent a qualitative widening which continued in the most recent round (Uruguay Round). This latest round saw the world trading system extend from trade in goods to embrace cross-border trade in services and protection of intellectual property rights - with the system being institutionally embedded in an umbrella World Trade Organization (WTO).

Table 1: GATT Rounds and Issues Negotiated

First Round	Geneva 1947 Tariff reduction - average 20 percent. Bilateral negotiations between the contracting parties.
Second Round	Annecy 1949 Additional tariff reduction - between 1 and 2 percent of the total. Ten additional signatories: Denmark, Dominican Republic, Finland, Greece, Haiti, Italy, Liberia, Nicaragua, Sweden and Uruguay.
Third Round	Torquay 1950/51 Defence of Commonwealth preferences by the United Kingdom, resulting in the other contracting parties withholding concessions. Additional signatories: Austria, Federal Republic of Germany, Korea, Peru, the Philippines and Turkey.
Fourth Round	Geneva 1955/56 No further progress on the liberalization of world trade. Japan signs the Agreement.
Fifth Round	Geneva 1961/62 (Dillon Round) New tariff negotiations following the establishment of the EEC and the fear that this would lead to regional tariff discrimination. The results of the negotiations were modest. Agreement signed by Cambodia, Israel and Portugal.
Sixth Round	Geneva 1964-67 (Kennedy Round) US proposed a new Round as a response to the growing importance of the EEC. Further tariff reductions of between 30 and 40 percent. Non-tariff barriers not addressed; no liberalization of agriculture. First multilateral negotiations.

Seventh Round	Geneva 1973-79 (Tokyo Round)
	Further reduction of about 35 percent of the remaining tariffs. Agreement reached on international treaties to cover grain, dairy products and bovine meat. Codes finalized to cover the areas of anti-dumping, subsidies and government procurement. Adoption of the Enabling Clause according special and differential treatment/preferences to the less-developed countries (non-industrial countries).
Eighth Round	Geneva 1986-93 (Uruguay Round)
	Deepening and widening of the existing GATT provisions: Tariff reduction, elimination of non-tariff trade barriers, improved access for agriculture, restructuring of the Agreements on Textiles and Clothing, Trade-Related Investment Measures, Rules of Origin, Anti-Dumping, Subsidies, etc. Revision of some individual GATT provisions dealing with state enterprises and safeguard clauses.
	Extension of the GATT to cross-border trade in services (General Agreement on Trade in Services, GATS), and protection of intellectual property rights (Trade-Related Aspects of Intellectual Property Rights, TRIPS).
	Creation of the World Trade Organization (WTO) as the umbrella organization for the GATT, GATS and TRIPS.
	Conclusion of the eighth round in Geneva on 15 December, 1993 and signature of the Agreements in Marrakesh on 15 April, 1994. Entry into force of the Agreements on 1 January, 1995.

1.5 Current Scope of Application of the WTO

GATT in its original form remained a fraction of the aborted ITO, a provisional treaty without an organization, restricted to trade in goods. Over the years GATT has grown in stature and scope, thanks to the addition of a number of areas with corresponding regulations and additional agreements; this, however, has been without achieving a final complete configuration. Qualitatively it could be said that the seventh and eighth rounds contributed most to GATT. These resulted in tariffs being reduced, non-tariff barriers being eliminated, the inclusion of cross-border trade in services and the protection of intellectual property rights and the transformation of the existing GATT into a trade organization, the World Trade Organization (WTO).

The following table indicates those areas which now fall within the scope of application of the WTO - in one form or another, as well as those areas which remain to be tackled.

Table 2: Scope of Application in line with the Final Act of the Uruguay Round*

Institutional Aspects

- WTO contribution to a greater economic policy convergence

- Creation of a comprehensive trade policy monitoring system

- Provision of an integrated dispute settlement procedure

- Trade and environmental protection (not yet completely worked out: given to WTO Preparatory Committee)

- Measures in favour of the non-industrial countries and the net food-importing non-industrial countries

---

I   Trade in Goods (GATT)

- Protocol on the consolidated reduction of tariffs and non-tariff barriers to trade (including primary products and tropical goods)

- Regulation of agriculture including phytosanitary measures

- Agreement on Trade in Textiles and Clothing

- Amendment of the Codes from the seventh round (Tokyo Round) - anti-dumping, technical barriers to trade, import licensing, subsidies and countervailing duties, notification commitment and valuation for customs purposes, civil aircraft**, government procurement**, dairy arrangement*** and arrangement regarding bovine meat***

- Revision or new interpretation of GATT provisions on customs tariffs and other charges, state enterprises, balance of payments measures, safeguard clauses, customs unions and free trade zones, waivers (treaty exemptions), amendments to tariff concessions and suspension of GATT rules in certain instances

- Agreement reached on rules of origin

- Regulation of preshipment inspection

- Agreement on trade-related investment measures

II   Trade in Services (GATS)

- Agreement on trade in services including a number of ministerial Decisions and Declarations on the institutional organization, the services-specific elements in the dispute settlement procedure, protection of the environment, labour mobility, financial services, air transport, telecommunications, international auditing and the audio-visual sector

III   Intellectual Property Rights (TRIPS)

- Agreement on Trade-Related Aspects of Intellectual Property Rights including trade in counterfeit goods and pirated copies

*	Text as per Agreements and Declarations
**	Only applicable for ratifying countries
***	Terminating December 1997

The Uruguay Round allowed two objectives to be achieved. Firstly, a wide range of separate agreements were consolidated within one text, referenced one to the other and clarification reached on their legally binding status. Secondly, an umbrella organization, with a uniform dispute settlement procedure, has been created.

2.   The WTO as an Institution

The WTO is the institutional framework for the world trading system which has emerged from the negotiations. It has its own organs with relevant decision-making powers, activities to be pursued and responsibilities for their implementation. As an overall organization, the WTO deals with the monitoring of trade policy, dispute settlement, protection of the environment, and measures in favour of the non-industrial countries as well as those dependent on primary products. The General Agreement on Tariffs and Trade (GATT) is an integral part of the WTO - together with all those agreements concluded under the umbrella of the GATT, the General Agreement on Trade in Services (GATS) and the Agreement on the Trade-Related Aspects of Intellectual Property Rights (TRIPS). In addition to the agreements which have been signed by all Members, there are individual treaties (on Civil Aircraft, Government Procurement and international trade in Dairy and Bovine Meat Products) which only apply to those countries which have ratified them, the latter two terminating in December 1997.

The following section gives an overview of the WTO membership and of the individual organs of the WTO, together with its decision-making and dispute settlement procedures.

2.1. Membership

The transfer of the original GATT (also known as GATT 47) to the WTO meant that the majority of the GATT contracting parties became Members of the WTO. Of the 125 countries involved in the multilateral trade negotiations (MTN) of the Uruguay Round, 111 signed the Agreements in Marrakesh. With the accesion of the Republic of Congo on 27 March 1997, all GATT contracting parties are now WTO Members (WTO, FOCUS, Newsletter No. 19, May 1997, p. 2). At the time of writing (October 1997) the WTO has 132 Members with 32 countries (observer governments) having applied for membership of the WTO. These applications are currently being considered by accession working parties. Among the countries currently involved in accession negotiations are Algeria, Cambodia, People's Republic of China, Panama, Russian

Federation, Saudi Arabia, Ukraine and Vietnam. The contracting parties to the original GATT - which have accepted the Final Act of the Uruguay Round and the international trading agreements negotiated under its auspices - are the founding members of the WTO. Those countries which carry the UN definition of least-developed countries (LDCs) are relieved of the treaty commitments and concessions to the extent consistent with their economic, financial and trade needs, or their administrative and institutional capabilities allow.

Countries which were not GATT 47 contracting parties but which had wanted to sign the Final Report of the Uruguay Round had first to negotiate their accession to GATT before they could sign the Final Act. The Uruguay Round Final Act as it now stands is not yet definitive for these countries. Full implementation remains to be tackled on a case by case basis within the process of the accession negotiations. Accession of a new WTO Member requires a two-thirds majority of all WTO Members.

All Members have the right to withdraw from the WTO. This can follow on foot of six months' notice to do so, in writing. The treaty permits Members to denounce individual additional treaties (plurilateral trade agreements) without leaving the WTO. The time limits involved in this are dealt with in the individual treaties.

A number of countries have denounced the GATT: these included the People's Republic of China (1950), Lebanon (1951), Liberia (1950) and Syria (1951). The People's Republic of China has enjoyed observer status since 1984 and was also involved in the MTN of the Uruguay Round as has been pointed out it is currently pursuing full membership of the WTO.

An overview of the geographical distribution and the development stage of individual WTO Members is shown below. It should, however, be borne in mind that it is often not possible to be precise as regards the division between industrial countries and non-industrial countries.

Table 3: Contracting Parties to GATT 47 and WTO

	Total		Industrial Countries		Non-industrial Countries	
	1948	1997	1948	1997	1948	1997
Europe *)	8	28	8	28	-	-
North America	2	2	2	2	-	-
Latin America	2	25	-	-	2	25
Africa	2	46	1	1	1	45
Asia	7	28	-	1	7	27
Oceania	2	2	2	2	-	-
Total	23	131	13	34	10	97

*) Including the East European Countries.

The increased number of European countries is largely due to the changed political landscape in Central and Eastern Europe, for example Members now include Hungary, Poland, Romania and Slovenia. The former USSR and its successor states were not GATT contracting parties nor have they acceded to the WTO as of yet although accession working parties have been established in many cases. Clearly the relatively modest foreign trade of the former USSR and the difficulty of reconciling a planned economy with international free trade were at the root of the non-accession of the USSR. In many instances accession of the non-industrial countries came about after they had achieved independence. It is estimated that world-wide between 70 and 80 percent of cross-border trade in goods and services is carried on by WTO Members.

2.2 Individual Organs

Because of the failure of the ITO, GATT 47 did not have a fixed organizational structure. The institutional development into an organization came about in the first instance thanks to the operation of customary law. This resulted in the extension of the General Agreement on Tariffs and Trade on the grounds of actual practice (Benedek, 1990: 185). The highest decision-making body was comprised of those countries which had signed the GATT as a treaty, the contracting parties. Their delegates met once a year under the name of CONTRACTING PARTIES, and they decided on the operation of the Agreement. Each contracting party was entitled to one vote. Amendments to MFN and the decision-making process required unanimity. The remaining areas - depending on importance - required a two-thirds majority of all contracting parties, or of those present and voting, or, if the Agreement was silent on the issue, a simple majority. In 1960 the CONTRACTING PARTIES devolved their competence to a large extent to the GATT Council to take over the day-to-day activities in the periods between the annual sessions of the CONTRACTING PARTIES. The GATT Council usually met once a month. The GATT Secretariat was in Geneva, headed by a Secretary-General of the CONTRACTING PARTIES, known as Director-General from 1965 onwards. Those who have held this office to date were: *Eric Wyndham White* (1948-1968), *Oliver Long* (1968-1980), *Arthur Dunkel* (1980-1993) and *Peter Sutherland* (1993-1995). Mr. *Sutherland* served briefly as the first Director-General of the WTO. *Renato Ruggiero* took over the office in 1995. Committees (standing) and working parties (ad hoc) were established to deal with individual problem areas (for example the question of trade in textiles and in agriculture). In the event of alleged violation of the Agreement the matter could be referred to a Dispute Panel which prepared a proposed solution for the GATT Council.

The WTO has taken over the basic structure of the GATT organization, adding two more Agreements to the existing GATT instruments - the Agreements on Trade in Services and on Trade-Related Aspects of Intellectual Property Rights. The following table shows the organizational structure of the WTO as set out in the Final Report of the Uruguay Round dated 15 April 1994.

Table 4: WTO Structure

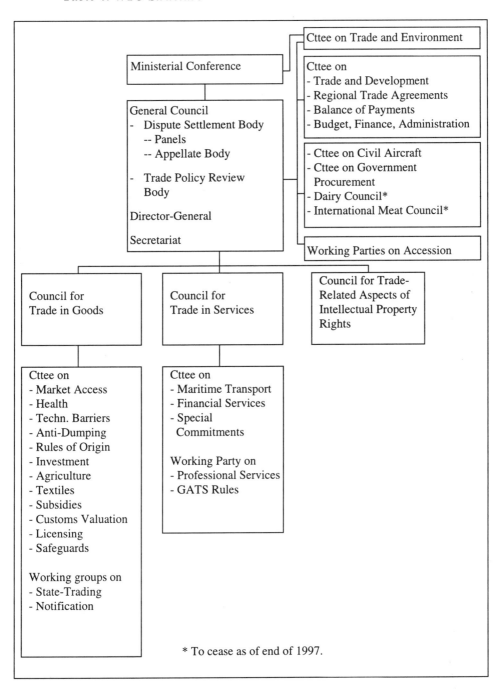

Ministerial Conference

Cttee on Trade and Environment

Cttee on
- Trade and Development
- Regional Trade Agreements
- Balance of Payments
- Budget, Finance, Administration

General Council
- Dispute Settlement Body
  -- Panels
  -- Appellate Body
- Trade Policy Review
  Body

Director-General

Secretariat

- Cttee on Civil Aircraft
- Cttee on Government
  Procurement
- Dairy Council*
- International Meat Council*

Working Parties on Accession

Council for
Trade in Goods

Council for
Trade in Services

Council for Trade-
Related Aspects of
Intellectual Property
Rights

Cttee on
- Market Access
- Health
- Techn. Barriers
- Anti-Dumping
- Rules of Origin
- Investment
- Agriculture
- Textiles
- Subsidies
- Customs Valuation
- Licensing
- Safeguards

Working groups on
- State-Trading
- Notification

Cttee on
- Maritime Transport
- Financial Services
- Special
  Commitments

Working Party on
- Professional Services
- GATS Rules

* To cease as of end of 1997.

Ministerial Conference: The supreme organ of the Organization is composed of the representatives of the Members at ministerial level meeting every two years. The Ministerial Conference carries the final responsibility for the functioning of the WTO. The first Ministerial Conference took place in Singapore in December 1996.

General Council: The General Council is responsible for carrying out the functions in the intervals between the regular sessions of the Ministerial Conference. Membership is composed of representatives of all the Members. The General Council meets once a month. Its role in the WTO is similar to that of the GATT Council within GATT 47. Because of its decision-making powers it is the most important organ of the WTO. Where in the following pages reference is made to the Ministerial Conference, this should be taken to apply equally to the General Council.

Director-General: The Director-General carries out the decisions of the Ministerial Conference and of the General Council and, at the same time, heads up the Secretariat. He has to prepare periodic reports on the activities of the WTO and also to present the annual budget estimate and financial statement to the Committee on Budget, Finance and Administration. He is appointed by the Ministerial Conference.

Secretariat: The main duties of the Secretariat are: to prepare and conduct negotiations between the WTO Members, advise the trading partners, prepare the analyses, presentation and publication of world trade developments and also assist in the dispute settlement process. The number of specialist professional staff in the legal, political, economic and statistics divisions of the WTO is approximately 450. By comparison, in other international organizations such as the IMF there are 1300, World Bank 3700 and OECD 1100. The Secretariat is located in Geneva.

Committees: In line with the Final Act of the Uruguay Round the Ministerial Conference has established the following Committees: the Committee on Trade and Development, the Committee on Regional Trade Agreements, the Committee on Balance of Payments and the Committee on Budget, Finance and Administration. The organization and working procedures of the Committees are the responsibility of the General Council.

Council for Trade in Goods, Council for Trade in Services and Council for TRIPS: As already mentioned the WTO extends to three main treaty areas: (1) The Agreements on Trade in Goods, known today as GATT 94. This is essentially the world trading system as established in 1947 (GATT 47) extended by the achievements reached in the Uruguay Round MTN in relation to agriculture, sanitary and phytosanitary (SPM) and other such measures, trade in textiles and clothing, technical barriers to trade, antidumping and subsidies, rules of origin, licensing and investment. In many instances what is involved is an extension of the Codes which emerged from the Tokyo Round, with the difference that these now apply to all WTO Members and not just to those states prepared to ratify them. (2) The Agreement on Trade in Services (GATS). (3) The Agreement on Trade-Related Aspects of Intellectual Property Rights, including Trade in Counterfeit Goods (TRIPS).

Each of these three trade areas has a standing working party: these are designated in the Final Act of the Uruguay Round as the Council for Trade in Goods, the Council for Trade in Services, and the Council for Trade-Related Aspects of Intellectual Property Rights. These Councils are responsible for the implementation of the individual agreements. The Councils are free to establish other bodies with a view to realizing their objectives. All Members are free to participate in the Councils. Council Chairpersons are elected by the Members.

2.3 Decision-Making Process

Each WTO Member has one vote when it comes to resolutions. The European Coomunities have votes equivalent to the number of their Member States which are WTO Members (Art. IX:I). In contrast to other international organizations - such as the IMF or the World Bank, the WTO does not employ any weighting - such as percentage of world trade held, contributions paid or other criteria - in the voting procedure.

All Members of the GATT, GATS or TRIPS have the right of initiative - in other words, all Members may put forward proposals.

As a continuation of existing GATT practice, the WTO attempts, wherever possible, to arrive at decisions based on consensus - of those present. There are special voting procedures in five areas:

- accession of new WTO Members
- interpretation of the provisions of the Agreement
- waiver of obligations
- amendment to the Agreement - and acceptance thereof
- amendment to core principles such as MFN and decision-making process

Any state or customs territory engaging in international trade is entitled to apply for WTO membership. Accession conditions are a matter for negotiation between the applicant state and the WTO Members. The final decision on accession is decided either by the Ministerial Conference or the General Council requiring a two-thirds majority. Those WTO Members which do not vote in favour of accession are not bound to acknowledge the new membership, just because of the two-thirds majority vote of the other Members.

The Ministerial Conference has sole competence to decide on the interpretation and application of the WTO Agreements, with a minimum of three-quarters of all Members in favour required for all decisions in these areas.

Members can be released from their WTO obligations in exceptional circumstances. The granting of a waiver normally requires a three-quarters majority of the Members. If it is a question of the release from an obligation which still remains unfulfilled on the expiry of the transitional period, unanimity is then required for the granting of a waiver. Currently applicable waivers expire on the expiry of the time allowed or, at the latest, two years after the entry into force of the WTO.

All WTO Members are entitled to propose amendments to the Agreements. With the exception of proposals to amend the core areas of MFN and procedural aspects - see below for these - the Ministerial Conference has a period of 90 days in which to arrive at a decision on the amendment of the rights and obligations of Members. A motion at ministerial level to amend the rights and obligations of Members requires a two-thirds majority of all votes. As has been the practice under GATT, a successful amendment is only legally binding on those states which have accepted it. One difference between the old and the new régimes is that the Ministerial Conference can exclude a country from the WTO if that country does not accept the amendment. This move requires a three-quarters majority of all Conference votes.

Proposals which do not amend rights and obligations of Members require a two-thirds majority of the Members too. These amendments bind all Members and not just those which vote in favour. The question of exclusion from the WTO does not arise in such instances.

Unanimity in the WTO Ministerial Conference is required in the event of proposals to amend the core principles of the WTO, such as MFN, national treatment and the decision-making process. Each Member enjoys the right of veto in these areas. There is no question of being excluded because of the exercise of this right.

The following table shows the decision-making process.

Table 5: Decision-Making Process

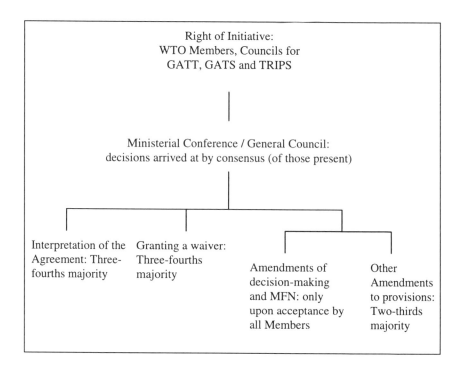

2.4 Dispute Settlement Procedure

The dispute settlement procedure as found in GATT goes back to 1952. At that time the CONTRACTING PARTIES established a working party to deal with any disputes arising. Subsequently the practice of establishing an expert group to deal with each case emerged. The legal basis for the panel process which had emerged through customary law is to be found in the 1979 description of the normal GATT practice (Benedek, 1990: 314 ff).

The current dispute settlement procedure is the result of the Uruguay Round, published as an interim report in Montreal in 1988 and extended by "The Uruguay Round Understanding on Rules and Procedures Governing the Settlement of Disputes" (GATT, Final Act, 1994: 353 ff). Because the Montreal provisions ran out in April 1994 appropriate measures were necessary in order to maintain their validity until the entry into force of the results of the Uruguay Round.

GATT has handled some 200 disputes. Of the complaints 27 percent were withdrawn in the course of the proceedings, 31 percent ended with conciliation between the parties and 42 percent were actually decided on. Nine tenths of the decisions arrived at were recognized by the parties to the dispute. The parties refused to accept the outcome of the panel deliberations or to remedy the treaty violation in the case of one tenth (for a statistical evaluation of the panels' deliberations see Hudec, 1993).

While the existing dispute settlement procedure was confined to trade in goods, the Uruguay Round introduced an extension to this. It now covers services, protection of intellectual property rights, civil aircraft and government procurement (as well as dairy and bovine meat products until the end of 1997). As far as specific Agreements (anti-dumping, technical barriers to trade, textiles, etc.) are concerned, the general dispute settlement procedures apply in so far as, and to the extent that, there are no special provisions in the Agreements themselves. There are numerous exemption clauses which apply to the non-industrial countries.

As far as the institutional aspect is concerned, compared with the earlier situation, the WTO dispute settlement process has been strengthened in that a permanent Dispute Settlement Body (DSB) and an Appellate Body have been set up.

The stages of the process are:

- In the event that Member A feels that its treaty rights have been impaired or violated, then A has the right to appropriate consultations with Member B. Member B is obliged to reply to country A within 10 days and within 30 days to engage in consultations with country A.

The DSB is kept informed on the commencement and progress of the consultations.

- If after 60 days there are no consultations between A and B, or if B refuses to enter into consultations, then A has the right to seek the setting up of a panel by the WTO. In urgent cases, consultations can be required within ten days, and in cases of refusal to engage in consultations, a panel can be requested after 20 days. Normally the panels have three members, none of whom comes from the countries concerned. If one of the parties to the dispute rejects a panel member (for example, on the grounds of alleged prejudice for one reason or another), it is up to the Director-General to arrange a new panel within 60 days. The WTO Secretariat maintains a list of potential panel members.

- WTO procedures require the dispute panel to present a report within six months or, in urgent cases, within three months. The report of the panel is neither final nor binding. It is in effect a proposal for the WTO Dispute Settlement Body, one of the working parties of the General Council.

- The report of the panel is considered as adopted if the DSB does not unanimously reject it within 60 days and none of the parties to the dispute lodges a protest. This is undoubtedly the most important de-velopment as regards the existing procedure in terms of increasing the legal status of the dispute panel.

- The WTO dispute settlement procedure allows any party to the dispute to appeal to the Appellate Body. Any such appeal must be limited to issues of law covered in the panel report and the legal interpretation as developed by the panel.

- Three members (a "division") of the seven person Appellate Body sit at any one time to hear an appeal. They can uphold, modify or reverse the legal findings and conclusions of the panel. As a general rule, the appeal proceedings are not to exceed 60 days but in no case are they to exceed 90 days.

- The time limit for adoption of the report by the DSB is within 30 days of it being issued. This must be unconditionally accepted by the parties to the dispute - unless there is a consensus against its adoption (WTO, Newsletter, FOCUS Jan./Feb. 1996, no. 8 p 3).

- After adoption of the report the party concerned is obliged to inform the DSB of the steps it intends to take to conform to the treaty. The DSB will monitor the implementation of reports. The dispute settlement procedure should be completed within nine months, or in the event of an appeal, within twelve months.

- In the event of a Member not implementing the panel's report, the injured party is entitled to approach the DSB and to seek to carry out retaliatory measures against the offending party - which has either not accepted or not implemented the panel's instructions. WTO law requires that the counter-measures should be in the same trade area as the violations shown. If this should not be possible, then counter-measures may be carried out in other areas (cross retaliation). The counter-measures should be proportionate and retaliation should cease at the same time as the violations cease.

The following table shows the dispute settlement procedure schematically:

Table 6: The Panel Process

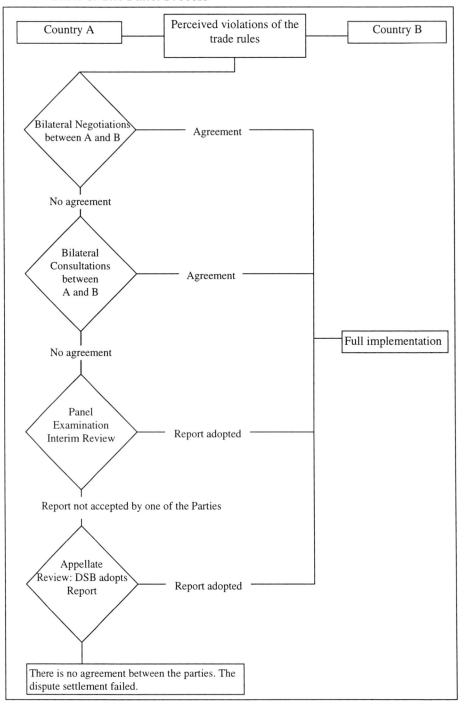

3. General Provisions

The various treaties and agreements of the WTO can be divided into two classes: there are the multilateral treaties which bind all WTO Members, and there are the plurilateral agreements which bind only the ratifying parties.

The multilateral treaties which are binding on all WTO Members can be further subdivided into two types. One type encompasses provisions which apply to all agreements, over and above specific treaties: that is, they apply to trade in goods and services and to the protection of intellectual property rights (MFN, national treatment, reciprocity, etc.). The other type covers measures which apply only to trade in goods, only to trade in services or only to the protection of intellectual property rights.

The plurilateral agreements, which are binding only on the ratifying parties, include the Agreements on Civil Aircraft, Government Procurement, Dairy Products and Bovine Meat. As has already been indicated, the latter two will terminate at the end of December 1997.

The following table shows the individual agreements according to their binding character and subject matter.

Table 7: Survey of the WTO Agreements

Multilateral Trade Agreements

GATT	GATS	TRIPS

General aspects

- Object
- Most-Favoured-Nation clause MFN
- National treatment
- Reciprocity
- Reduction of trade barriers
- Special treatment of non-industrial countries
- Protection of environment

GATT	GATS	TRIPS
Agriculture	Movement of Natural Persons	Transitional Arrangements
Health	Air Transport	
Textiles/Clothing	Financial Services	
Techn. Barriers	Telecommunications	
Investment		
Dumping		
Customs Valuation		
Preshipment		
Rules of Origin		
Import Licensing		
Subsidies		
Safeguards		

Plurilateral Trade Agreements

- Civil Aircraft
- Government Procurement
- Dairy Agreement (deleted as of end of 1997)
- Bovine Meat Agreement (deleted as of end of 1997)

The generally applicable trade provisions apply over and above the individual specific Agreements for the GATT, the GATS and the TRIPS and the plurilateral agreements. These basic principles existed to a large extent in GATT 47 and have now been enshrined in the WTO Agreement and/or the multilateral agreements - GATT, GATS and TRIPS. These are the common objectives of the WTO, the principle of MFN, national treatment for goods, services and intellectual property rights, reciprocity, provisions on the elimination of trade barriers, preferences for the non-industrial countries and protection of the environment.

3.1 Common Objectives

A comparison between the objectives of GATT 47 and those of the WTO does, however, highlight a new direction. GATT 47 referred to "raising standards of living, ensuring full employment and a large and steadily growing volume of real income and effective demand, developing the full use of the resources of the world and expanding the production and exchange of goods". The Preamble to the WTO Agreement omits "developing the full use of the resources of the world" and instead joins the raising standards of living and the ensuring of full employment with the requirement of "optimal use of the world's resources" in harmony with sustainable development, which both protects and preserves the environment as well as enhancing the means to achieve this. Consequently the world trading system has undergone a change in direction, with the environment becoming a determining factor.

In addition to the inclusion of the environment in the Preamble to the WTO Agreement, there is a new section on the special consideration required to address the needs of the non-industrial countries. The WTO Members recognize the necessity of guaranteeing an appropriate share of world trade to the non-industrial countries - especially the least-developed countries - commensurate with the needs of their economic development. In order to protect the interests of the poorer countries, provision is made for the setting up of a Committee on Trade and Development within the framework of the WTO. One of the tasks of this Committee will be to monitor the activities of the WTO from the point of view of the non-industrial countries and to submit regular reports to the WTO General

Council. In addition it will prepare proposals for improving the situation in these countries.

3.2 Most-Favoured-Nation Principle

What is the principle of Most-Favoured-Nation (MFN)? In which areas is it applied? What are the forms of exemptions?

Principle

Article I of GATT 94, article II of the GATS and article 4 of the TRIPS all employ more or less the same terminology. This is to the effect that WTO Members are obliged to accord all advantages, favours, privileges and immunities which they accord to another country, or a national of another state in relation to trade in goods, services or as regards intellectual property rights immediately and unconditionally for like goods, services and intellectual property rights, to all other WTO Members and their nationals. It is irrelevant whether or not the country concerned is a WTO Member or whether the national concerned is a national of a WTO Member. In other words, WTO Members may not treat other WTO Members differently, nor may they disadvantage them vis-à-vis third countries. On the other hand, every country is free to decide whether it will accord the advantages enjoyed by WTO Members to non-member countries.

In contrast to the big trading blocs such as the US and the EU, which sometimes use the principle of MFN as a weapon of trade policy - for example against the former USSR and the People's Republic of China - the small countries accord MFN to all countries, including non-contracting parties.

The use of the word "immediately" (to be accorded) in the text of the Agreement indicates that the advantages, favours etc. are to be accorded to all WTO Members at the same time and without any time lapses. There is no question of these being accorded to one country after another.

"Unconditionally" means that the favours are to be accorded to all WTO Members without further consideration in return or any additional conditions. The reference to "unconditionally" is a deliberate move away from the practice, as seen in the 1920s, in which concessions were only granted to third countries if they were prepared to provide a *quid pro quo*.

Scope

The principle of Most-Favoured-Nation covers:

- the amendment of customs duties and charges of all kinds which arise in relation to the import and export of goods and services

- international transfer of payments for imports or exports

- the method of levying customs duties and other border charges

- the administrative procedures in relation to the recording and control of cross-border movements in goods and services

- the levying of goods and services with direct or indirect charges

- the legal regulation of trade, sales, transport, distribution and use of imported goods and services within the national territory

- the regulation of the intellectual property rights in the form of standard procedures, regarding counterfeiting, copyright and patents.

The two Agreements on services and intellectual property do not deal with services and intellectual property rights *per se* but rather with their providers. The emphasis is on nationals of WTO Members who provide cross-border services, who for the purpose of providing a service reside in another country (Member), or who are represented in another country (Member) by one means or another (for example, by an agent).

The application of MFN has been the subject of much discussion over the years. The question of "like product" has been raised in many panel decisions. For example, in a case involving Spain in 1979, the Spanish authorities did not impose any customs duties on the importation of roasted coffee (from Colombia) whereas they imposed 7 percent customs duties on unroasted coffee (from Brazil). Their argument was that roasted and un-roasted coffee were different products. Rejecting the existing practice of the dispute panels, the GATT panel came to the decision in this case, that it was a matter of "like product". It is not usual that the taste or the aroma of the end product distinguishes the basic item, quite apart from the fact that the end usage of the product, as a drink, was the same. On this basis, any difference in levying customs duties as between roasted and unroasted coffee was to be seen as a violation of "like product" (see BISD 28S/111 f).

In contrast to this, the GATT panel did not regard the requirement of minimum prices in relation to the import of tomato extracts as a violation of the Most-Favoured-Nation clause. So long as these minimum prices applied to all suppliers, it was of no significance for GATT that it was easier for centrally planned economies to comply with these measures than it is for those countries pursuing free trade policies (see BISD 25S/68 ff).

It is impossible to draw a line once and for all under the debate on the question of "like products". Depending on the interests concerned - different criteria are applied. For example, in dealing with timber should the decisive criterion be the biological species, the intrinsic quality of the product or end usage? Trees of the same species produce quite different timber quality depending on whether they are grown at a temperate sea level or in northern climes in poor mountain areas. Should the deciding factor be the type of tree, the quality of the timber or the potential usage? (see the Dispute over timber export from Canada to Japan, GATT, Focus 1989/62 June, p 1 ff).

Exemptions

The MFN principle is not watertight, partly because of the exemption provisions in the original GATT and partly because of the concessions granted afterwards in the additional Agreements. Among the exemptions provided for in the Agreement are the provisions allowing for the creation of customs unions, free trade areas or contiguous frontier zones, as well as the guaranteeing of preferences in favour of the non-industrial countries. The Multifibre Agreement (MFA) contains a range of concessions as do the Codes from the 1970s and 1980s.

The most important exemption to MFN is the regulation in GATT which provides for the creation of customs unions and free trade areas, with a view to facilitating trade between the participating countries without any negative effects for other (third country) trading partners. GATT describes a customs union as "the substitution of a single customs territory for two or more customs territories" in which the trade restrictions on substantially all the trade between the constituent territories are eliminated and substantially the same duties and other regulations are applied within the GATT towards third countries. In line with this, new customs and trade restrictions vis-à-vis non-Members may not "in their totality (be) higher or more restrictive" than the general level of customs duties and trade restrictions before the creation of the common area. The GATT defines a free trade area as "a group of two or more customs territories in which the duties and other restrictive regulations of commerce are eliminated on substantially all the trade between the constituent territories in products originating in such territories". The countries comprising the free trade area retain their individual customs duties vis-à-vis third countries. The relevance of customs unions and free trade areas can be seen from the following figures: the EU currently enjoys 22 percent of world trade (excluding intra trade), NAFTA has 14.2 percent and EFTA has 8 percent. Trade between EU Member States is of the order of a quarter of world trade, between the NAFTA ratifying states it is between 5 and 6 percent and EFTA enjoys approximately 1 percent of world trade (Senti, 1994: 18).

The GATS also has an important exemption to the MFN principle. The Agreement allows the Members to create contiguous frontier zones in which adjacent countries guarantee each other advantages aimed at facilitating the exchange of services. In addition, when the Agreement on Services entered into force, the individual Members could draw up Schedules of the exemptions required for their country. Altogether 61 such Schedules were deposited with the WTO when the WTO entered into force.

The requirement for preferential treatment in favour of non-industrial countries goes back to the time of the extension of the GATT Agreement in the 1960s (Part IV of GATT) and to the UNCTAD Conference held in 1964. During the Tokyo Round, the GATT contracting parties decided to take a fresh approach to regulating both the existing, and anticipated preferential treatment in favour of the non-industrial countries. This led to the 1979 Enabling Clause adopted by the contracting parties. This ensures that preferential treatment in favour of non-industrial countries conforms to GATT. "Notwithstanding the provisions of Article I of GATT, contracting parties may accord differential and more favourable treatment to developing countries, without according such treatment to other contracting parties" (BISD 26S/203). The Enabling Clause relates to: (1) Preferential tariff treatment in accordance with the Generalized System of Preferences. The Generalized System allows the industrial countries to import semi-finished and finished goods from the non-industrial countries free of tariffs. (2) Non-tariff barriers - in the form of subsidies, anti-dumping provisions, rules on government procurement and licensing. (3) Preferential treatment in relation to tariffs between the non-industrial countries. Trade between these countries at the moment is of the order of 1 to 2 percent of world trade. (4) Special treatment of the non-industrial (least-developed) countries, such as the granting of specific import quotas.

A further important exemption is to be found in the MFA - which is an integral part of the GATT - in its current form. The MFA requires the contracting parties to regulate cross-border trade in textiles on a multilateral basis. However, in the event of a "real danger of irretrievable breakdown of the market" the Agreement permits - in certain circumstances - the conclusion of bilateral agreements. Prerequisites for this are the maintenance of existing trade volumes and preferential treatment for the non-industrial countries. The current Agreement covers some 80 percent of world trade in textiles. With a view to enhancing free trade and MFN, a new Agreement was concluded within the framework of the Uruguay Round: this new Agreement on Textiles and Clothing anticipates bringing the trade in textiles within the GATT fold on a phased basis over the next ten years. (See section 4.4 d which deals with the Agreement on Textiles and Clothing).

3.3 National Treatment

A second core area of the WTO world trading system is the principle
of national treatment. This obliges the Members to treat manufacturers,
goods and services from other Member countries the same as local manufacturers, goods and services. Tariffs are excluded from this. If a country
does need foreign protection then tariffs are seen as the appropriate route.
This exception is based on the view that tariffs are reasonably transparent
and easily administered as an instrument of foreign trade policy, whereas
non-tariff barriers are usually difficult to monitor.

The Most-Favoured-Nation clause has been extended by the application of the principle of national treatment as a principle of non-discrimination between WTO Member countries to cover the relationship between
foreign WTO Member countries and the country concerned. MFN can be
seen as a prohibition on discrimination horizontally between WTO Members, whereas national treatment is a vertical prohibition on discrimination
between WTO Members and the country concerned.

The main provisions dealing with national treatment are to be found
in article III of the GATT, article XVII of the GATS and article 3 of the
TRIPS. There are differences between the provisions of GATT, GATS and
TRIPS in that each of these regulates different areas of trade - GATT deals
with goods, GATS addresses services and providers of services and TRIPS
deals exclusively with the protection of the right holder, his nationality,
residence and domicile.

In the General Agreement on Tariffs and Trade (GATT), the WTO
Members have accepted that "internal taxes and other internal charges, and
laws, regulations and requirements affecting the internal sale, offering for
sale, purchase, transportation, distribution or use of products internally as
well as internal quantitative regulations requiring the mixture, processing
or use of products in specified amounts or proportions should not be
applied to imported or domestic products so as to afford protection to domestic production". This broad formulation provides an inexhaustive list of
non-tariff trade barriers.

The text of the Agreement goes on to allow both for a restriction and also for a widening of the national treatment principle: the restriction arises from the application of the principle of no less favourable treatment of "like products". (The difficulty of arriving at a definition of "like product" was dealt with in the last section). The widening is to be found in that "moreover" internal taxes or other internal charges are not to be applied in a manner contrary to principles outlined above. This means - as *John H. Jackson* showed in relation to the 1948 treaty negotiations - that not only the less favourable treatment of "like" but also of "competing" products is prohibited. A country which has no indigenous orange production violates GATT if it imposes such high tariffs that the consumption of oranges reduces and consumers turn to apples (Jackson, 1969: 282).

National treatment does not apply to laws, regulations or requirements governing the procuring by governmental agencies of products purchased for governmental purposes and not with a view to commercial resale or with a view to use in the production of goods for commercial sale. The GATT national treatment provisions do not prevent the payment of subsidies to domestic producers. This also applies as regards payments to domestic producers derived from the proceeds of internal taxes or charges applied in accordance with the provisions of GATT, and subsidies effected through governmental purchases of domestic products.

The General Agreement on Trade in Services (GATS) obliges the Members to accord no less favourable treatment to services and providers of services from other Member countries than accorded to the same domestic services and service providers. National treatment applies, however, only to those services which are recorded in the Schedules drawn up by the WTO Members and deposited with the WTO. The Agreement speaks of a no less favourable treatment when the non-national service or service provider is disadvantaged competitively, that is, in its competitive position vis-à-vis domestic services or providers of services. As was seen in relation to goods, the question of definition of "like offer" is an extremely difficult one. Just as is the case with goods, it can be seen both as the actual "like", as well as a substitute or competitive service.

National treatment does not apply to services which are procured by governmental agencies for governmental purposes and not with a view to commercial usage.

The principle of national treatment is also to be found in the TRIPS. This is a continuation of the basic principle of equal treatment to be found in earlier international treaties. The 1967 Paris Convention states that the nationals of a ratifying party enjoy the same protection of intellectual property rights in all contracting parties "which the relevant laws guarantee for their own nationals either now or in the future" (SR 0.232.04). Similar wording is to be found in the Berne Convention (SR 0.232.14).

3.4 Principle of Reciprocity

An additional key aspect of the WTO Agreements is the principle of reciprocity. This basic principle - to be found in GATT 47 - goes back to the 1934 US Trade Act. The "Reciprocal Trade Agreements Act" empowered the US President to reduce tariffs on imported goods from those countries which were prepared to offer equivalent concessions to products of US origin.

Reciprocity in this context should be understood in a political sense. Political reciprocity arises in relation to negotiations and can be distinguished from legal reciprocity in that this is provided for in both the GATT and the WTO by means of MFN.

Within the framework of GATT the political principle of reciprocity applies to tariff negotiations (article XXVIII[bis]) and emergency action (article XIX:3). Negotiations on the reduction of tariff levels are to be conducted on "a reciprocal and mutually advantageous basis". Protective measures adopted against unforeseen developments arising as a result of the effect of obligations - including tariff concessions - incurred by a contracting party must be "balanced" and "equivalent". The non-industrial countries are the only ones from which the GATT does not expect reciprocity for tariff reductions or the elimination of other trade barriers.

Similar to the GATT MTN Rounds, the new GATS anticipates MTN in relation to the reduction and elimination of trade barriers in international trade in services. According to article XIX of the GATS the negotiations are to proceed on a mutually advantageous basis for all participants, with a view to securing an overall balance of rights and obligations. Account is to be taken of the state of economic development in individual countries, with particular emphasis on the non-industrial countries.

The principle of reciprocity is also found in the TRIPS. According to article 7 of TRIPS, promotion of technological innovation, transfer and dissemination of technology should take place in a manner conducive both to social and economic well-being, and to a balance of the rights and obligations of the contracting parties.

The principle of reciprocity is based on the following arguments :

- Terms of Trade: If trade in goods takes place between two countries whose tariffs influence the terms of trade, the terms of trade can only be retained by both sides reducing tariffs by the same amount. Every country is concerned to observe reciprocity to the extent that the terms of trade are not thereby changed to its disadvantage.

- Employment: Each party to the negotiations is concerned to ensure that those workers who become unemployed as a result of job losses stemming from easier imports should find new employment opportunities created by increased exports. This particular argument always assumes greater importance in times of high unemployment.

- Balance of payments: Every country endeavours to ensure that its balance of payments situation is improved in the course of negotiations, or at the very least, does not deteriorate.

- Negotiations: The principle of reciprocity allows the individual parties to the negotiations to include demands for export advantages to be extended to products which otherwise would not have been the subject of negotiations. What this means in practice is trade policy compensation activities, whereby demands in relation to one product group are paid for by concessions in other trade areas.

- Justification: In the final analysis the delegates involved in the negotiations have to convince their governments, parliament and even possibly the head of state. Sectoral interests and the social partners represent other concerned groups to be persuaded. They are therefore obliged, in their own interest, to conduct negotiations in such a way that the right balance is struck between what is conceded and what is won.

Currently there are signs of conflict as regards the retention of the principle of reciprocity. This is because individual countries and groups of countries are moving away from the negotiating principle of traditional reciprocity to a strategy of aggressive reciprocity.

According to GATT 47 the principle of traditional reciprocity requires that the negotiations relate solely to mutual, equivalent and balanced concessions without thereby endangering in any way the level of protection of any country. In GATT terminology one speaks of "mutually balanced lists" and "equivalent concessions". For example, the Kennedy Round demanded a mutual tariff reduction of up to 50 percent of existing tariff levels. Differing tariff levels could be retained by individual countries - on a country by country basis.

In contrast to the traditional forms of negotiations, new negotiating strategies have been evident in the US and the EU in the last twenty years. Under the heading of "fair" trade, the two parties demand the same market access conditions from their trading partners as they offer themselves. The reciprocity of the negotiations do not refer to the specific negotiating concessions but to the parity of market access. The newly drafted legislation provides the governments and administration with the means to bring about adequate market access with the aid of appropriate means of coercion. This form of negotiation is described in the literature as aggressive reciprocity.

It remains to be seen, whether the renewed acknowledgement of traditional reciprocity, to be found in the Uruguay Round, can stem the practice of the strategy of aggressive reciprocity in individual countries and groupings of countries.

3.5 Elimination of Trade Barriers

A specific feature of both the current and future world trading systems is the reciprocal reduction of trade barriers. There is a certain unevenness in the approach in that tariffs are merely to be reduced, whereas non-tariff barriers, on the other hand, are to be fully eliminated. This approach is accounted for, and justified, in different ways. One argument is that every country has the right to protect its own interests. Protection, however, should be based on measures which are as transparent and accountable as possible. This applies to a greater extent to tariffs than to non-tariff barriers. The latter can take the form of administrative sleights of hand or quantitative restrictions and can be applied arbitrarily. The emphasis of the GATT on tariffs may also be rooted in the past. Retaining customs duties while at the same time eliminating the non-tariff barriers underlined the wish to bring back the "golden days before the First World War", when tariffs represented the sole trade barriers. Non-tariff barriers were too reminiscent of the First World War period and the ensuing world-wide economic crisis. In addition, the negotiating sub-groups involved in the creation of a new world trading system were only too conscious that the founding Members were not prepared to eliminate all tariffs. The same also held true for the non-tariff barriers. The difference here, however, was that the negotiating parties were fully aware that effective control was not possible.

The distinction between tariff and non-tariff barriers has found its way both into the literature and into the trade negotiations and is also now a fixed point in the landscape of international trade policy terminology. Nevertheless it must be remembered that a division of trade barriers on the basis of tariff affiliation is meaningless, whether as a legal description or in relation to its effect on foreign trade. It is irrelevant for the importer whether the charges levied at the border are in the form of a customs duty or a tax, as an additional payment added to the price, or as a compulsory charge, as an import deposit, or administrative additional fee, etc. This is quite apart from the fact that taxes and other charges equivalent to customs duties also exist in the form of laws and regulations. That this terminological differentiation has been able to become established - especially since the Kennedy Round - has its roots in the fact that tariffs allow relatively simple country-by-country comparisons. This is largely because of the uniform product classification in the customs tariffs and the widely and commonly agreed methods of calculation. This contrasts with the extremely difficult task of trying to compare differing taxation systems, price additions, standards, procedural provisions, etc., and endeavouring to arrive at a common denominator.

The following pages will address the question of tariff reduction and move on to the elimination of the non-tariff barriers.

Reduction of Tariffs

It has always been the case that tariffs have been at the centre of the GATT MTNs. At the beginning of the 1950s the average tariff level of industrial products (sum of the bound tariff rates divided by the number of positions) worked out at between 40 and 50 percent of the import value. This sank to 6.3 percent during the first seven MTN rounds. In the Uruguay Round a further reduction to an average of 3.9 percent was achieved. The average tariff rates after the Uruguay Round (see table 8 below) were of the order of 12.1 percent for textiles and clothing, 7.3 percent for leather and rubber goods, 5.8 percent for means of transport, etc. The tariff level for agriculture will only be known when each country has carried out the tariffication (transposing the non-tariff trade barriers into tariffs).

Table 8: Tariff Reductions during the Uruguay Round

Product category	Import value in billions of $	Average tariff in %		
		Pre	Post	Reduction
Industrial products	736.9	6.3	3.9	38
Textiles and clothing	66.4	15.5	12.1	22
Leather, rubber, footwear	31.7	8.9	7.3	18
Transport	96.3	7.5	5.8	23
Chemicals	61.0	6.7	3.9	42
Electrical appliances	86.0	6.6	3.5	47
Fish and fish products	18.5	6.1	4.5	26
Metals	69.4	3.7	1.5	59
Mineral products	72.9	2.3	1.1	52

Source: GATT, News of the Uruguay Round, April 1994: 11.

In its original form, GATT represented, to a large extent, a document on the results of the tariff negotiations. The tariff concessions were bound in Schedules. Being bound meant that these tariff rates could only be lowered further, and could not be raised without concessions being accorded to other countries. The rate of tariff binding for manufactured products from the industrial countries rose during the Uruguay Round from 78 to 99 percent (trade-weighted from 94 to 99 percent), those of the non-industrial countries from 22 to 72 percent (14 to 59 percent) and the applicable figures for the transition economies (reforming Central and East European countries) from 73 to 98 percent (74 to 96 percent). The reports of the negotiations show that before the Uruguay Round, North America and Europe had adhered almost 100 percent to established binding rates. Latin America raised its binding from 38 to 100 percent (57 to 100 percent) whereas, Asia, as before, held back and raised its binding only from 17 to 67 percent (36 to 70 percent) (see GATT, News of the Uruguay Round, April 1994, p 7). Prior to the Uruguay Round, tariffs for agriculture were not bound. Following the Uruguay Round they are to be fully (100 percent) bound. It is important to note, as far as bilateral trade relations are concerned, that the GATT/WTO principles (MFN, national treatment, etc.) also apply to non-bound tariffs.

In article XXVIII[bis] the GATT contracting parties recognize "that customs duties often constitute serious obstacles to trade; thus negotiations on a reciprocal and mutually advantageous basis, directed to the substantial reduction of the general level of tariffs and other charges on imports and exports and in particular to the reduction of such high tariffs as discourage the importation even of minimum quantities, and conducted with due regard to the objectives of this Agreement and the varying needs of individual contracting parties, are of great importance to the expansion of international trade. The CONTRACTING PARTIES may, therefore, sponsor such negotiations from time to time". What does the GATT mean by tariffs? How do they relate to the Schedules?

The GATT usage of the term "tariffs" is wide in that reference is made to "duties and other charges" and encompasses all border charges between the contracting parties and between GATT contracting parties and third countries. In reality, however, GATT has been concerned exclusively with the duties set out in the tariffs and not with the "other charges".

Duties falling into the fiscal category are excluded by GATT. According to GATT, a contracting party can impose a similar internal charge on imports, so long as this charge does not give the domestic product some advantage. Petroleum and automobiles are among those goods which mainly attract fiscal charges in individual countries. Further exceptions are the anti-dumping and subsidy-related countervailing duties which are allowed by GATT, as well as the fees and other charges arising for services rendered.

It was possible within the framework of the Uruguay Round to reduce the rates of duty on manufactured and industrial products by a further 38 percent. For the industrial countries this meant the arithmetical duty fell from 6.3 to 3.8 percent and the average tariff level calculated on trade volume fell from 4.7 to 2.9 percent. There is the perception that high tariffs undergo a greater reduction - relatively speaking - than those which are already low. Import duties on steel, pharmaceutical products, drinks, paper and toys disappear completely. Tariff reductions are about 60 percent in Japan; in Canada, the European Communities and USA around 50 percent; in Australia, New Zealand and South Korea approximately 40 percent, and in the Latin American countries 25 to 30 percent. The tariff reduction is effected in five equal annual amounts to run from the date of the entry into force of the WTO Agreements. However, the parties are free to reduce tariffs earlier (ifo Schnelldienst 1-2/1994: 3).

Elimination of Non-Tariff Barriers to Trade

Articles III, VIII and XI of the GATT require that non-tariff barriers be eliminated. Despite this, however, right up to the second half of the 1960s this failed to appear among the issues to be addressed during GATT negotiations. Given the heterogeneity and changeability of this type of trade barrier, the feasibility of engaging in common negotiations was questioned. In addition, there was the legal question: could non-tariff barriers - which were contrary to the GATT - be the subject of reciprocal negotiations?

The extent and diversity of non-tariff barriers became very clear when inventory lists were drawn up by GATT in the 1960s and 1970s.

Table 9: List of Non-Tariff Barriers to Trade

Group I

Subsidies
State trading
Government procurement
Anti-competitive measures

Group II

Consular formalities
Dutiable values provisions
Anti-dumping duties
Customs formalities
Customs tariffication

Group III

Industry, health, safety and other standards
Packaging, labelling and rules of origin

Group IV

Quantitative restrictions and import licences
Embargoes and other restrictions
Film quotas
Discrimination based on bilateral treaties
Currency controls
Measures to regulate domestic prices
Export restrictions
Discrimination against suppliers
Customs quotas
Other restrictions

Group V

Additional charges, port and statistical fees
Border compensation tax
Discriminatory film tax
Pre-arranged import deposits
Variable levies
Emergency measures

Source: Presse- und Informationsdienst der deutschen Bundesregierung, No. 43,
          22.4.74.

It is extremely difficult - if not impossible - to calculate the extent of the protectionist effect of non-tariff barriers. Many of the methods resorted to by the authorities do not lend themselves to being measured: examples would be pressure to substitute imported goods with domestic products or standards provisions. At the same time, *Robert E. Baldwin* shows that, for example, after the Kennedy Round, a third of the actual protectionism in the USA - taking the effects of the trade barriers on semi-finished goods and value-added elements into consideration - was related solely to export subsidies and indirect taxes. Compared to the 1950s, the actual protectionism showed an upward trend - because of the non-tariff trade barriers - partly as a result of the tariff reduction arrived at during the Kennedy Round, but partly also because of higher indirect taxes (Baldwin, 1970: 165). It can be assumed that, considering the non-quantifiable barriers, the actual trade restrictive effect of the non-tariff measures is equal to that of tariffs, although, however, there may be a wide range of differences between the various countries.

The 1967 Anti-Dumping Code was the first GATT Agreement on non-tariff barriers. The Tokyo Round also saw the emergence of Agreements on valuation of goods for customs purposes, licensing and standards. The Agreements on subsidies, government procurement and the technical barriers to trade were concluded by the negotiating committee on behalf of the governments in 1979.

The elimination of the non-tariff barriers was a prime objective of the Uruguay Round. The result - unlike tariffs - cannot be detailed in Schedules, but is to be found in the inclusion of services and intellectual property in the WTO as well as the widening of the anti-dumping, subsidies and agricultural provisions (see the relevant sections).

3.6 Consideration of Non-Industrial Countries

In 1948 the GATT was composed of thirteen industrial countries and ten non-industrial countries. The current WTO membership has approximately one-third industrial countries while the remaining two-thirds are non-industrial countries. Despite the poor countries having a numerical majority, the industrial countries (whose share of foreign trade represents about 80 percent of world trade) remain the major players in the WTO.

The conflict of interest between North and South was apparent, even at the time of the drafting of GATT in the 1940s. While some problems could be tackled, others continued to persist. An analysis of the economic situation in the poorer countries at the end of the 1950s (Haberler-Report) led in 1966 to a widening of the General Agreement on Tariffs and Trade to include Part IV "Trade and Development". This Part contains the general objectives and principles on the development of the non-industrial countries without infringing normative provisions. There was one exemption and that was in the readiness of the industrial countries to forego the principle of reciprocity vis-à-vis the poorer countries. In the 1960s, the non-industrial countries demanded, in addition, preferential market access from the industrial countries. The guarantee of the preferences came about in the Tokyo Round in the form of an "Enabling Clause". This allowed the industrial countries to accord the non-industrial countries "differential and more favourable treatment" without having to accord this preferential treatment to other GATT contracting parties.

There are also exemptions in favour of the non-industrial countries in the special Agreements, (Safeguard Action for Development Purposes Decision of the Tokyo Round), as well as in the Agreements on services and intellectual property rights.

Exemptions from the Most-Favoured-Nation Principle

The 1979 Enabling Clause (of the Tokyo Round) allowed the non-industrial countries to avail of preferential treatment which did not have to be accorded to other contracting parties. This exemption applied to tariffs, non-tariff barriers and the creation of regional or global arrangements between poor countries. Currently most industrial countries accord the non-industrial countries tariff free market access for manufactured and industrial goods. Agricultural products are usually excluded from this preferential treatment.

Possible Waiver of the Principle of National Treatment

The GATT allows the non-industrial countries to change, or even increase, the bound tariffs found in the Schedules in accordance with their own calculations, and without the agreement of the other contracting parties, in order to promote their own industrial base. In addition, the poorer countries may take other kinds of safeguard measures for reasons other than balance of payments deficit, if the other contracting parties agree to these changes.

Release from Reciprocity

As required by GATT the "developed" contracting parties do not expect anything in return in negotiations with the "less-developed" contracting partners. However, the Tokyo and Uruguay Rounds have relativized this release from reciprocity for the non-industrial countries. This means that countries with more advanced economic development have to increase their participation in the rights and obligations of the WTO. This allows the reciprocity debate to be based on the ability of the countries concerned to adjust their economic, financial and administrative structures and performance.

Special Status in Additional Agreements

The contracting parties acknowledge that countries whose economies allow only a low standard of living, and which are only at the early stages of their development, may initiate measures which are actually contrary to the WTO provisions. This special treatment is to be found primarily in the multilateral Agreements, which, following the entry into force of the WTO are binding for all countries, including the non-industrial countries. For example, the Subsidies Agreement maintains that non-industrial countries may retain state support as part of their economic development programmes; or that in applying anti-dumping measures the industrial countries have to give special consideration to the special position of the poorer countries. The only plurilateral Agreement of interest in this regard is the Agreement on Government Procurement which has not been signed by the non-industrial countries.

Apart from the fact that the WTO only imposes obligations on the poorer countries to the extent that their economic, financial and administrative capabilities allow, these countries enjoy the benefit of an extra year's grace before having to provide their Schedules of concessions and obligations. The extension of this period for non-industrial countries is similar to guaranteeing a transitional period (although, however, the period of one year may not be exceeded).

3.7 Protection of the Environment

GATT 47 ignored any policy regarding the environment as it is understood today. Countries are entitled - on the basis of the general GATT exceptions - to protect their environment. Measures referred to as "measures to protect human, animal or plant life or health" as well as "measures relating to the conservation of exhaustible natural resources." may be taken. At the same time GATT does not prohibit the improper attack on, or destruction of, the environment within a Member's own country (see article XX of GATT). No particular concern for the environment emerged during the Tokyo Round.

The increased number of disputes referred to the GATT dispute settlement procedure is a clear indication that the existence of the general exceptions to GATT, and the possible exemption provisions, (exemptions which require a three-quarters majority in the Ministerial Conference/General Council), were insufficient to resolve the world-wide problems of the environment.

Among the questions raised repeatedly in recent years have been:

- May tuna fish imports be prohibited from one country when the supplying country has engaged in overfishing and as a consequence contributed to the "exhaustion of natural resources"?

- Is a country permitted to impose special import duties on petroleum and petroleum products in order to use the proceeds to clean up areas destroyed by toxic waste?

- May a country prohibit the export of unprocessed herrings and salmon based on the argument that otherwise the demand would be so big that fish stocks would be endangered?

- May foreign cigarettes incur an additional levy at the border on the basis that foreign tobacco products are more dangerous to health than domestic products?

- Can the prohibition on the importation of tuna fish and tuna fish by-products from one country be justified because these have been landed with drag nets which also kill dolphins?

(For an overview of the individual dispute panel decisions see Diem, 1996: 24 ff; and Petersmann, 1993: 43 ff).

The current state of the law is such that the WTO does not oppose the protection of the domestic environmental products in whatever form, so long as the measures in question do not produce discriminatory effects. Charges are allowed on domestic production and on imported goods, so long as they are not abused (effectively by protecting the domestic industry).

Current WTO law does not allow *expressis verbis* measures for the extraterritorial protection of the environment (in whatever aspect). The WTO supports non-interference in extraterritorial matters relating to the environment. This is based on the belief that to allow unilateral measures to protect the non-national environment is to give free rein to arbitrary action and to question the existing (sought after) certainty and predictability of the world trading system. "This strict point of view is consistent within the meaning of the GATT basic consensus approach but it inhibits a mutually satisfactory balance between free trade and effective protection of the environment" (Beise, 1993: 3, translated).

As a consequence of the MTN in the Uruguay Round and Marrakesh the WTO does seem to be taking on a somewhat "green tinge" (Beise). The new WTO instruments have references to the environment: in the WTO Preamble (optimal use of world resources in accordance with the objective of sustainable development, which protects and preserves the environment); in the Agreement on Agriculture, Annex 2 (payments permitted to protect the environment); in the Agreement on the Application of Sanitary and Phytosanitary Measures, article 6 (Pest or Disease Free Zones); in the Agreement on Technical Barriers to Trade, article 2 (measures permitted to protect the environment); and in the Agreement on Subsidies, article 8.2c (support of environmental requirements). Similar references are to be found in the GATS (article XIVb) and in TRIPS (article 27.2).

In addition to the provisions which apply to all the WTO Agreements, there are special regulations for the international trade in goods, cross-border trade in services and the protection of intellectual property rights.

4. General Agreement on Tariffs and Trade

GATT 94 is made up of GATT 47 as amended by the Uruguay Round, as well as the additional Agreements on Agriculture, Sanitary and Phytosanitary Measures, Textiles and Clothing, Technical Barriers to Trade, Trade-Related Aspects of Investment, Anti-Dumping, Customs Valuation, Subsidies and other trade areas. The following is an overview of the special provisions of GATT, supplemented by individual presentation of the additional Agreements.

4.1 GATT Provisions

The GATT consists of the generally applicable treaty provisions as detailed in section 3 as well as some provisions specific to trade in goods. The following provides a brief outline.

- GATT 47 requires the contracting parties to "bind" their mutually negotiated tariff concessions in Schedules and to submit these to the GATT. Bound tariffs may not be amended or increased without fresh negotiations. During the Uruguay Round it was agreed that in future "other levies and charges" would also be bound. As a result, these may not be changed unilaterally in order to protect the domestic economy. The new Schedules apply with the entry into force of the WTO. The GATT permits concessions to be renegotiated at intervals of three years. As a first step, negotiations are to be conducted with the principal supplying interest, with the understanding that after five years' experience, the decision can be taken as to the appropriate approach to be followed.

As can be seen from table 10, the industrial countries have bound 99 percent of their tariffs as opposed to 59 percent for the non-industrial countries and 96 percent for the countries in transition.

Commentaries on the Uruguay Round negotiations indicate that many non-industrial countries have bound their tariffs over the actual coverage level. This means that in future they will be able to increase their tariffs within the framework of the binding. The positive impression given by the overview should therefore not be regarded as a full picture.

Table 10: **Pre- and Post-Uruguay Round Scope of Bindings for Industrial Products (excluding petroleum)**

Country group or region	Number of lines	Import value in billions of $	Tariff lines bound in %		Imports under bound rates in %	
			Pre-	Post-	Pre-	Post-
By major country group:						
Industrial economies	86,968	737.2	78	99	94	99
Non-industrial economies	157,805	306.2	22	72	14	59
Transition economies	18,962	34.7	73	98	74	96
By selected region:						
North America	14,138	325.7	99	100	99	100
Latin America	64,136	40.4	38	100	57	100
Western Europe	57,851	239.9	79	82	98	98
Central Eastern Europe	23,565	38.1	63	98	68	97
Asia	82,545	415.4	17	67	36	70

The data on non-industrial economies cover 26 participants; those 26 participants account for approximately 80 per cent of the merchandise imports, and roughly 30 per cent of the tariff lines, of the 93 non-industrial-country participants in the Uruguay Round.

Source: GATT, News of the Uruguay Round, April 1994: 7.

- GATT allows individual contracting parties to protect their national film industry. This can be done by prescribing playing time for films produced domestically and establishing playing time quotas for foreign films. In measuring foreign quotas the MFN prohibits, in particular, divisions based on supplier countries. The European countries - and France in particular - were successful in the Uruguay Round in opposing a liberalization of the film, multimedia and television areas.

It is difficult to judge whether this protectionism benefits the culture or the industry which creates them.

- The contracting parties have mutually agreed to allow free transit for "goods, vessels and other means of transport" with the exception of aircraft. This means that there can be no difference in treatment arising from the flag state of the ship, ownership of the goods or source, origin or destination. This does not mean that there are no customs formalities. The charges levied must be confined to the actual costs for the services rendered. They may not act as indirect protection for domestic products, nor form part of an internal taxation system to contribute to state revenue. This restriction on charges applies not only for transit traffic but also for imports and exports.

- In the event that a country experiences balance of payments difficulties, or runs the risk of losing its currency reserves, it is entitled to protect its financial situation by restricting imports. This can be done either by means of quantitative restrictions or by applying a value ceiling. The measures chosen should not violate the basic WTO principles (MFN, national treatment, reciprocity, etc.) and any restriction on international trade should be confined to what is strictly necessary. There has been a debate for some years as to whether these GATT provisions have any relevance in a system of floating exchange rates.

- A further chapter of GATT is devoted to state trading. State trading is the term employed when the state or individual organs of the state control cross-border trade in goods to a large extent and exert a decisive influence on the price of the goods or the quantities to be traded. State measures to regulate state trading are only justified if they do not violate the objectives of GATT and the basic principle of non-discrimination. GATT obliges the state enterprises established by the contracting parties to conduct purchases and sales exclusively in line with commercial considerations and to afford other trading partners adequate opportunity to compete for participation in the sales and purchases. There are three areas where a contracting party is released from the obligation of non-discrimination: (1) import of goods for own use (this does not fall under state trading but comes within government procurement); (2) imports funded by loan for this purpose; (3) price differentiation in exports where, however, the differentiation in prices arises from commercial considerations.

4.2 Agreement on Agriculture

The main provisions of the new Agreement on Agriculture can be divided into three areas: (1) improved market access at the international level or reciprocal improved market access to agricultural markets; (2) the restriction and restructuring of domestic support mechanisms, and (3) the improvement of international competition by a reduction of export subsidies and subsidized export quotas.

Market access

The objective of market access is pursued within the traditional spirit and meaning of the GATT. This means possible retention of domestic border protection - regarded as necessary from the national perspective - applied in the form of tariffs, with, at the same time, the elimination of non-tariff barriers (NTBs). This requires a transformation of the quantitative restrictions, variable import charges (variable adjustment levies), minimum price provisions, import licences, state trading measures and voluntary trade restrictions into legally binding tariffs.

In order to change the NTBs into tariffs - a process known as tariffication - it is necessary to collect data on a widespread basis and then to make the appropriate calculations. Basically the new tariff arises from the difference between the average domestic price and the foreign reference price for the years 1986/88. The foreign reference price is the price of the product at the border inclusive of carriage, insurance and freight (c.i.f.).

The tariffs which result from tariffication, together with the existing tariffs, are to be reduced on average by 36 percent, running over a period of six years from the entry into force of the Agreement, with a minimum of 15 percent per product. Undoubtedly individual countries will structure their tariff reductions so that the tariffs for those products for which there is no, or only very modest, domestic production are reduced by more than

36 percent, in order to be able to have a lesser tariff reduction for more sensitive products. For the non-industrial countries the applicable tariff reduction is 24 percent (two-thirds of 36 percent) over ten years. The least-developed countries are exempted from tariff reduction. The existing Schedules act as the reference point for calculation (for bound tariffs) or else the customs duty level applicable on 1 September, 1986 (for non-bound tariffs).

Tariffication of NTBs, as well as the retention of import opportunities at the same level as for 1986/88, requires that the existing quantitative re-strictions (quotas) be capable of being changed into tariff quotas. This means that quantities imported during the reference period of 1986/88 are to be levied at the levels of charges applicable at that time. Additional im-port quantities are possible - in contrast to volume quotas. However, these attract the new tariff based on the difference between the domestic and foreign price. It is up to each country to regulate the division of the tariff quotas among the importers.

Additional market access is required by the WTO at the same time. For products which up to this point were excluded - wholly or in part - from imports, there should be market access of at least 3 percent of the average total demand of 1986/88 during the first year of the transitional period, followed by an increase to 5 percent by the end of the six-year reform period.

As is the case with GATT 47, the new agricultural system has safe-guard provisions for those cases where the easing of imports leads to an excessively steep increase in the volume of imports or to an import price slump.

The volume-based safeguard provisions allow an increase in the existing duty level up to a third in the event of the import volume in any one year exceeding a particular trigger level. It should be noted that "up to a third" has not been more clearly defined.

There is a different trigger level applicable for each country, depend-ing on the extent to which that country is self-sufficient and on the volume of imports. The trigger levels for levying a safeguard duty are set according to the following schedule:

- where the level of self-sufficiency is 90 percent and import volume 10 percent, (and) if the additional imports stand at more than 25 percent over the average volume of imports during the three preceding years for which data are available,

- where the level of self-sufficiency is 70 percent to 90 percent and import volume 10 percent to 30 percent, (and) if the additional imports amount to more than 10 percent of the average volume of imports during the three preceding years for which data are available,

- where the self-sufficiency level is less than 70 percent and volume of imports over 30 percent, (and) if the additional imports amount to more than 5 percent over the average imports during the three preceding years for which data are available.

If, in the course of the comparison period, there is an increase in the level of self-sufficiency vis-à-vis total domestic consumption, there is an increase in the trigger level corresponding to the additional domestic production, which equals a reduction of the safeguard level. For example, if domestic production amounts to 80 units (self-sufficiency level) and imports 20 units, the trigger level is of the order of 110 units. If imports increase from 20 to more than 30 units, the trigger level of 110 will be exceeded, allowing the imposition of countervailing duties. If the level of self-sufficiency increases at the same time, say by ten units, the increased domestic production increases the trigger level by ten units and intervention can only occur from the 120 trigger level. Taking imports to date into account, together with the change of the self-sufficiency level, has a number of consequences. There is a longer period before safeguard measures can be invoked, where smaller import volumes are concerned; longer, that is, than where there are already bigger volumes of imports. In addition, an extension of the self-sufficiency level is related to the increase in the trigger value. This seems to reward the existing market access and to penalise increased domestic production. GATT 94 is silent on the issue as to whether the relevant volume and price changes are economically based and justified (for example as a result of increased productivity).

If the guaranteed tariff reductions lead to a price slump in import trade and consequently exert a knock-on effect on the domestic market, the country in question has the right to impose counter-measures related to the extent of the price reduction.

There are in total five levels with the price-related safeguard provisions, imposed according to the following schedule:

- less than 10 percent decrease in the import price: no temporary additional duty

- 10 to 40 percent decrease in the import price: additional levy of 30 percent of the price difference so long as it amounts to more than 10 percent

- 40 to 60 percent decrease in the import price: additional levy of 50 percent of the additional price difference

- 60 to 75 percent decrease in the import price: additional level of 70 percent of the additional price difference

- more than 75 percent decrease in the import price: additional levy of 90 percent of the additional price difference

If, for example, the import price of a product drops by 80 percent, the importing country can levy a safeguard duty of 34 percent of the price decrease (in addition to the already existing duty) (existing duty + no additional levy for the first 10% = 0 + 30% of 30% = 9.0 + 50% of 20% = 10 + 70% of 15% = 10.5 + 90% of 5% = 4.5. Together: 9.0 + 10 + 10.5 + 4.5 = 34.0% in addition to the existing duty).

Table 11: Special Safeguard Provision for Import Price Changes

Import price decrease in %	Permitted additional duty	Example: Import price decrease of 80% (cf. text)		
0 - 10	0	0% of 10%	=	0%
10 - 40	30	30% of 20%	=	9.0%
40 - 60	50	50% of 20%	=	10.0%
60 - 75	70	70% of 15%	=	10.5%
over 75	90	90% of 5%	=	4.5%
		Total additional duty permitted: 34.0% in addition to the existing duty.		

Restructuring of the Support Mechanisms

The second objective of the WTO Agreement on Agriculture is the restriction and restructuring of domestic support of agriculture in such a fashion that foreign trade and production are either not at all, or only very slightly, influenced. In concrete terms, the WTO requires the reduction of all product-related supports (price and marketing support measures as well as product-related direct payments) by 20 percent on the basis of 1986-88 figures. The reduction applies globally - that is, to all products. Excluded from the reduction are product-specific state supports which are less than 5 percent of the individual product value, and non-product-specific supports of less than 5 percent of a country's total agricultural production. The limit is 10 percent for non-industrial countries. Restrictions do not apply to supports which, because of existing production restriction programmes, do not lead to an expansion of agricultural production and which are paid out of public funds, that is to say, are not directly imposed on the consumer. Also exempted from reductions is the so-called "Green Box". Included in this are mainly regional, socio-political and ecologically motivated measures such as (1) government programmes to support agriculture or rural/agricultural areas in general. Included here are i.a. research, control of food-stuffs, education, supervision, marketing and infrastructural programmes, (2) payments for obligatory stockholdings to be available in the event of outbreak of war or other emergencies as laid down in national legislation, (3) food aid programmes for needy sections of the population, (4) direct payments and compensation payments to producers to compensate for loss of income. However, these payments may not be related to the level of production, national or international prices or the means of production used. The range of exemptions is so wide and varied that every country will be able to support its agriculture as in the past - albeit in line with a different system (via non-production-related amounts) and certainly involving considerably greater administrative expense.

Reduction of the Export Subsidies

A third aspect of the Agreement on Agriculture provides for the reduction of export subsidies and subsidized exports. According to the Agreement, export subsidies include direct payments (by governments or their agents) to exporting producers, processors and traders, government sale of agricultural surplus at prices lying below the domestic level, as well as transport supports to agriculture. The WTO requires a reduction of agricultural subsidies of the order of 36 percent, taking 1986-90 as the base period, to be achieved over a period of six years, running from the entry into force of the Agreement. The non-industrial countries are required by the WTO to reduce their subsidies by 24 percent (two-thirds of 36 percent) over a period of ten years. Subsidies for transport costs are not regarded as forming part of those subsidies to be reduced by the non-industrial countries. Least-developed countries are exempted from the requirement to reduce subsidies.

The volume of subsidized exports is to be reduced by a total of 21 percent over the same period of six years running from the entry into force of the Agreement. The figure for non-industrial countries is 14 percent (two-thirds of 21 percent). In the event that exports increase after the base period of 1986-90 - both in terms of value and volume - 1991-92 can be be substituted instead, without affecting the period of subsidy reduction. The reduction of 36 percent in export subsidies also applies to processed foods and consequently, to the food industry. Processed foods are not subject to any quantitative reduction.

Problems of Enforcement

Among the declared objectives of the WTO Agreement on Agriculture is the establishment of a fair (and market-oriented) international trading system in agriculture. As far as possible, this should be free from trade barriers and export subsidies: it should take particular account of the position of the non-industrial countries and the need to ensure supplies of food and to protect the environment. Arising from this, there is a fundamental change of system, a new framework for the future agricultural policy. Instead of income-related product prices there should be market prices, supplemented by income-securing direct payments to those engaged in agriculture. The realization of the new agricultural market system worked out during the Uruguay Round will cause considerable difficulties in most countries. The reasons for this are to be found in the enormous difficulties which will emerge from the calculation of the new tariffs and tariff quotas, as well as the distribution of the quotas and direct income payments - caused by missing data and the lack of political decisions. In addition, ongoing discussions show that there are considerable differences both between the different economic interest groups (production, processing and trade) and among producers, processors and traders (for example, among animal feed producers, pork and poultry fatteners). Depending on the point of view of the interest group involved, the fairly generous room for manoeuvre provided by the Agreement will be regarded either as an opportunity or as a threat. It should be borne in mind that quite possibly the new situation to emerge may not be any more transparent, with less bureaucracy - whether nationally or internationally - or any less dependent on the public purse than has been the case hitherto. The danger does exist that market access, the reduction of support mechanisms and the improvement of international competition may well be accompanied by complicated new regulations and exemption clauses, full of loopholes and unforeseen snares. It remains to be seen.

4.3 Agreement on the Application of Sanitary and Phytosanitary Measures

The Agreement on the Application of Sanitary and Phytosanitary Measures is to a large extent a reformulation and a refinement of the general exceptions in article XX of GATT.

The Preamble and the first part of the text set out that all Members have the right to protect human life and health, as well as animal or plant life and health. This is subject to the requirement that these measures are not applied in a manner which would constitute a means of arbitrary or unjustifiable discrimination between Members, or place non-national suppliers of goods or services at a disadvantage vis-à-vis domestic suppliers.

The second part of the Agreement deals with cooperation between the WTO Members and the harmonization of measures. The Members are required to harmonize their measures on as wide a basis as possible and to base them on international standards, guidelines and recommendations. In addition, the Agreement expects the Members to play a full part in the relevant international organizations and subsidiary bodies. Specific mention is made of the Codex Alimentarius Commission, the International Office of Epizootics and the regional organizations operating within the framework of the International Plant Protection Convention. The task of promoting and co-ordinating the co-operation between the individual Members and the international institutions is devolved to a Committee.

A further provision requires for the acceptance, as equivalent, of non-national sanitary and phytosanitary measures, if they do not breach the national level of protection. According to the Agreement, the realization of this provision allows the importing country to inspect the product - as well as other relevant procedures - in the exporting country.

The trading partners may enter into bilateral or multilateral agreements, dealing with recognition of the equivalence of specified sanitary and phytosanitary measures.

Only if there are particular risks and the measures concerned can be justified scientifically may measures be taken, which, as far as safety is concerned, lie over the internationally recognized levels. The following factors are taken into account in assessing the risks: potential damage in terms of loss of production or sales, costs of control and possible alternative programmes.

The Members are obliged to take account of the special needs of the non-industrial countries. According to the Agreement this means taking the following into account: technical assistance in the form of technology transfer, scientific and financial support for research and establishment of national regulatory bodies, providing for lengthy transitional periods for the introduction of new measures, and assisting in the contribution to international committees.

Disputes are to be referred to the DSB. A Committee on Sanitary and Phytosanitary Measures is responsible for information and consultation. This Committee is entrusted with carrying out the functions necessary to implement the provisions of the Agreement.

The Agreement entered into force at the same time as the WT0, for the industrial countries. For the non-industrial and least-developed countries it will enter into force five years later.

4.4 Agreement on Textiles and Clothing

The international textiles trade has been characterised for years by stiff competition. From a very early stage in the post-war period, numerous voluntary export restraint agreements began to emerge aimed at protecting the home textile industry from cheap imports from countries such as Japan, India, Egypt, Spain and Portugal. With a view to curtailing this market distortion, the Permanent Textiles Committee (within the GATT) was given the task of elaborating proposals for an international agreement for the common regulation of trade in textiles. These endeavours led to the 1961 "Short-Term Arrangement Regarding International Trade in Textiles" which was signed by 19 countries, followed one year later by the "Long-Term Arrangement Regarding International Trade in Cotton Textiles

(LTA)" with a life span of five years, extended in 1967 and 1970. The Multifibre Arrangement (MFA) emerged in 1974 with the objective of tackling the existing trade restrictions. The MFA - which has been extended four times up to 1994 - prohibits the adoption of new import barriers and requires bilateral restrictions to be reduced by at least 6 percent annually: this obligation to liberalize is referred to in the literature as "development clause". Despite the best efforts of GATT over many years it is calculated that some 50 percent of trade in textiles and clothing is still subject to quantitative restrictions.

From the very beginning, it was the declared objective of the Uruguay Round to re-integrate trade in textiles (and thereby also the trade in cotton), which was disproportionately strongly regulated, into a market system in line with GATT. Arising from this, a new Textiles Agreement emerged in the course of the Uruguay Round negotiations - to enter into force concurrently with the WTO. According to this, the existing trade restrictions - based on the MFA - are to be phased out in four stages (the reference point is the 1990 import volume): (1) at least 16 percent on 1 January 1995; (2) at least a further 17 percent on 1 January 1998; (3) at least a further 18 percent on 1 January 2002; and (4) the remaining trade barriers are to be removed by 1 January 2005. At the same time, the Agreement requires that those remaining restrictions are to be liberalized by a certain percentage annually (16 to 27 percent). Similar to the existing methods employed to regulate the sector, the new Agreement allows the carrying over/forward of the previous year's unused quotas and the anticipation of future quotas. The carry overs and carry forwards together may amount to up to 10 percent of the permitted annual import quota.

Trade restrictions outside the framework of the MFA are to be eliminated where possible within the first year after the entry into force of the new Agreement, and at the latest, by the end of the ten-year transitional period.

The Agreement also contains a range of safeguard mechanisms, applicable in the event of a threat or damage to the domestic textile industry. If no amicable understanding is reached between the Members, the injured party has the right to take safeguard actions for, at most, three years; this may not result in a reduction in import quantities below the level of the previous twelve months. Import restrictions with a life span of more than one year are to be phased out at the rate of 6 percent annually. The Textiles Monitoring Body (TMB) is to be kept informed in all instances - with a view to arriving at an amicable understanding. If it should prove impossible to redress alleged infringements of the Agreement, each Member has the right to bring the dispute before the DSB.

Those provisions of the Agreement where the Members acknowledge *expressis verbis* that circumvention of the provisions of the Agreement by falsification of data or official documentation frustrates the implementation of the Agreement, and that Members are to take the necessary steps to fulfil their treaty obligations, seem somewhat extraordinary.

The Agreement provides for a Textiles Monitoring Body (TMB) to be established by the GATT Council (for Trade in Goods) with ten members and a Chairperson. Its activities include notifying the Members, providing advice, dispute settlement and preparing comprehensive reports on the implementation of the Agreement at least five months before the end of each stage, for transmission to the Council for Trade in Goods.

4.5 Agreement on Technical Barriers to Trade

It is impossible to conceive of a modern society without state provisions and standards directed at the protection of human, plant and animal life and health, and the environment. In addition to this, uniform standards and norms are necessary for an effective, functioning world trading system. The extent of state intervention in these areas differs from country to country - depending on the actual situation and the sensitivities involved. The world trading system envisaged in the WTO respects the right of self-preservation while at the same time seeks to promote a system of undistorted world trade.

In order to avoid the trade restrictive effect of technical regulations and standards, and with a view to improving co-operation between the individual contracting parties in the elaboration, adoption and application of technical requirements, an Agreement dealing with technical barriers to trade was concluded in the course of the Tokyo Round. This Agreement - reworked and extended - is now part of the new world trading system.

The Agreement differentiates between technical regulations, technical standards and specifications. The term technical regulation is taken to mean the agreement on product characteristics or their related processes and production methods, compliance with which is mandatory for all Members. The technical norm (also referred to as standard), on the other hand, is a technical product characteristic which is approved by a recognized body for common and repeated use, but compliance with which is not mandatory. The specification assessment of a product refers to the level of quality, the performance, the safety, the packing, the identification or the description of the product.

The objectives of the Agreement are: retention of MFN and the principle of national treatment, transparency of regulations and norms, cooperation between the Members, harmonization of the measures adopted and uniform dispute settlement procedure within the WTO framework.

Products imported from the territory of any Member may not be accorded treatment any less favourable than that accorded to like products of domestic origin, or to like products originating in any other country, as far as technical regulations and standards are concerned. The Agreement is deliberately couched in broad terms in order to encompass licensing requirements, monitoring methods and administrative measures, and not just the product itself. The principle of national treatment - as an extension of MFN - is to be observed. Recourse to technical regulations and norms should not be such as to give an advantage to domestic products or suppliers.

The Agreement places particular emphasis on the mutual provision of information by the Members. All Members are obliged to set up an enquiry point whose task will be twofold. It will provide information for non-nationals on current domestic regulations, on any conformity assessment procedures operated within its territory and on any administrative requirements. It will also provide information for domestic suppliers on technical regulations and standards applicable in other countries. If national regulations deviate from international standards, the country concerned is required to make this information available, in published form, via the WTO Secretariat.

The obligation to keep all concerned informed forms the basis for another objective of the Agreement, namely, co-operation between the Members. The Members are to provide mutual technical assistance, especially in the drafting of regulations, the establishment of national standardizing and regulatory bodies and bodies for the assessment of conformity with technical regulations. The industrial countries are required to take special account of the needs of the non-industrial countries. The Agreement addresses the question of co-operation between the national bodies and existing international organizations. This refers to the International Organization for Standardization (ISO), the Economic Commission for Europe (ECE), the International Electrotechnical Organization (IEC), as well as the FAO Kodex Alimentarius.

The international organizations are concerned primarily with the technical aspects of regulations and standards. The WTO, on the other hand, is concerned mainly with matters of trade in general. A further key aspect of the Agreement is the international harmonization of technical regulations and standards, in order to remove possible distortions to trade. The Members are required - within the limits of their economic and administrative capabilities - to participate in the harmonization of the technical regulations and standards, and in conformity assessment systems and administrative procedures. In addition, it is expected that in those instances where non-national regulations depart from domestic regulations in form only, but not materially, that these will be accepted. This is an indication of the attempt to promote mutual recognition.

In contrast to the earlier Agreement with its own dispute settlement procedure, the new Agreement provides for referral to the general dispute settlement procedures of the WTO (DSB). If one of the Members feels that its rights have been violated, it has the right to refer the matter to the WTO - and as an extension of the normal dispute settlement procedure - to request the establishment of a Technical Expert Group. The Technical Expert Groups are composed of technical experts drawn from individual Members (excluding the parties to the dispute) and will assist the DSB.

4.6 Agreement on Trade-Related Investment Measures

The world trading system, as encompassed by GATT 47, had no special provisions dealing with trade-related investments. The growth of international trade, and the increased importance of foreign investment and capital transfer connected with this, were among the reasons why the delegates to the Uruguay Round paid special attention to those investment regulations which were of a trade distorting or trade restricting nature. The outcome of the negotiations forms the new Agreement - the Agreement on Trade-Related Investment Measures (TRIMS).

The Agreement deals exclusively with investments which relate to the international trade in goods. Purely financial transactions or trade in securities, stocks, bonds and precious metals are not covered.

The two main objectives of the Agreement are the realization of the principle of national treatment and the prohibition of quantitative restrictions on imports - in relation to trade-related foreign investments. The Agreement prohibits trade-related investment measures which require the purchase or use of products of domestic origin, or the purchase or use of imported products, limited to an amount related to the volume or value of local products exported (principle of national treatment). Also prohibited are investment regulations which restrict imports as regards volume or value, or which link imports in relation to the volume or value of local production exported, or restrict access to foreign exchange to an amount related to the foreign exchange inflows attributable to the enterprise, or allow the export specified in terms only of volume or value of products related to a proportion of volume or value of local production (prohibition of quantitative restrictions on imports).

Within three months of the entry into force of the Agreement, the Members must notify the Council for Trade in Goods of all investment measures which are not in conformity with the Agreement. This notification obligation extends to notification of those organs of the national media which regularly carry details of the investment measures.

The industrial countries are to eliminate any of their investment measures not in conformity with the Agreement within two years. Non-industrial countries have a transitional period of five years and least-developed countries have a seven year period.

A Committee on Trade-Related Investment Measures will monitor the operation and implementation of the Agreement. The DSB will be the appropriate body to deal with the settlement of disputes.

4.7 Agreement on Anti-Dumping

During the debate on the restructuring of the world trading system after the Second World War, many delegates wanted to go beyond the then US approach of regulating price dumping and to include service, financial and social dumping in the new world trading order. In the end, agreement could only be reached on the price dumping in line with the US proposal. There were differences of opinion on the question of the extent of the injury required in order to justify the imposition of anti-dumping duties. Should it be a matter of a serious, material or an undetermined injury before anti-dumping duties be applied? Must the price difference between domestic price and export price reach a particular level (for example, 5 percent of the domestic price) before anti-dumping duties could be justified? Could a serious injury be countered by a criminal penalty? Should agreement be sought from the authorities before levying anti-dumping duties? In the end it was decided that anti-dumping duties may only be applied when the contracting parties determine that through dumping the effect "is such as to cause or threaten material injury to an established domestic industry, or is such as to retard materially the establishment of a domestic industry" (GATT, article VI:6a).

1955 saw the extension of this to include "where delay might cause damage which would be difficult to repair" which allows the levying of a countervailing duty without the prior approval of the CONTRACTING PARTIES.

The current provisions are drawn from the Anti-Dumping Code which emerged from the Kennedy Round, extended and revised in the Tokyo and Uruguay Rounds (Agreement on Implementation of Article VI of GATT 1994).

The anti-dumping regulation which emerged from the Uruguay Round is of enormous importance. This is because recent times have seen the tendency for various countries and groups of countries to use anti-dumping measures as a protectionist instrument. *Ludger Schuknecht,* in his research on trade protectionism, showed that for example in the 1980s the European Communities had over 900 anti-dumping cases. Three-quarters of all cases ended with "voluntary" price increases by the suppliers or with additional duties on the imported products (1992: 290 ff). The objective of the new Agreement is the more precise definition of anti-dumping, anti-dumping duties and the referral of disputes to the DSB.

Definition of Dumping

Harking back to the US legal philosophy of the 1920s and 1930s, the Agreement speaks of dumping when "like products" are introduced into the commerce of another country at less than their normal value.

Dumping therefore means that the normal domestic value of a product lies above its export value. How does the Agreement define "normal" domestic value? When is one product, compared to another product, "like"? What is to be understood under the term "export value"?

A product is to be considered as being introduced into the commerce of an importing country at less than its normal value

- when the export price of the product exported from one country to another is less than the comparable price, in the ordinary course of trade, for the like product for consumption in the exporting country. If there are no sales of the product in the exporting country:

- when the export price of the product in the ordinary course of trade is less than for the like product exported to a third country. If there are no sales of the product either in the exporting country or in a third country:

- when the export price of the product in the ordinary course of trade is less than the costs of production in the exporting country, together with a reasonable amount for administrative, selling and general costs and for profits.

Different selling arrangements and taxes, as well as other deviations impacting on the price, should be taken into account in an adequate way.

As regards the export price, this is to be taken as the price of the product on export and not the price at which it is imported; in other words, in the ideal case, the ex-factory price on sales for export.

Anti-Dumping Duties

Anti-Dumping Duties may be levied if two conditions are met:

- on determination of the existence of dumping

- on determination of injury or threat of material injury to a domestic industry/sector of the economy through dumping.

Having dealt with how the question of dumping is to be understood, it is appropriate to examine how GATT or the Anti-dumping Agreement define "injury", "threat" and "domestic industry".

For the purpose of determination of injury, the Anti-dumping Agreement requires an objective examination (1) of the volume of the dumped imports and the effect of the dumped imports on prices in the domestic market for like products, and (2) the consequent impact of these imports on domestic producers of such products.

In determining the volume of imports, consideration will be given either to the absolute, or the relative, increase in imports (for example, to market share in relation to the domestic production or domestic consumption in the importing country). In 1993, for example, the Canadians justified the levying of anti-dumping duties on US steel imports by reference to the increased market share for the US in Canada from 4.5 percent in 1986 to more than 16 percent in 1992.

In the same year the US used the same arguments to levy anti-dumping duties on steel imports from 19 countries including Japan, Brazil, Mexico and EU Member States.

In determining the price undercutting, emphasis is placed on whether the dumped imports have had a significant price undercutting effect as compared with the price of a like product of the importing country, or whether these imports have had a significant impact on the prices or have prevented a price increase by some means or other. For example, in the 1980s the European Commission established a dumping margin up to 70 percent on refrigerators from the Far East. The Anti-dumping Agreement is in no way absolute as regards determination of injury, it still contains quantifiable details on volume, price and effect of imports. The objective of the Agreement is rather more to unify the determination procedure and a call for fairer evaluation of the infliction of injury.

Anti-dumping duties may only be levied if a causal link between dumped imports and injury or threat (of injury) can be shown. All relevant factors are to be included in addressing the causal link - according to the Uruguay Round outcome - as now found in the Agreement. This would include, for example, imports which are not sold at dumping prices, changes in consumption or demand, changes in trade practices, technical developments, productivity of domestic production, etc. Anti-dumping levies are only justified if the injury and threat to a domestic industry or sector of the economy can be seen to stem from dumping imports. No anti-dumping duties are permitted if other factors are the cause of injury to domestic industry or sector of the economy. In practice, however, it is extremely difficult to adopt this clear division.

In line with the Uruguay Round outcome, an investigation is to be discontinued if the price difference between normal value and dumped price is less than two percent of the export price, or the trade volume concerned is less than three percent of the trade volume of this product area.

If the conditions permitting the levying of anti-dumping duties are met, the importing country has the right to demand provisional levies in the form of duties or cash deposit or bond, not earlier than sixty days after the beginning of the investigation and for not longer than four or - after an extension - six months. The charges levied may not exceed the price margin established.

In contrast to the former anti-dumping régime, the new Agreement has provisions on the duration of the anti-dumping levies. Basically, anti-dumping duties may only be levied while dumping is occurring. Notwithstanding this basic principle, definitive duties terminate after five years unless, before the end of that period, the relevant authorities determine that dumping is ongoing. It is necessary to institute a new investigation of the issues in order to determine that dumping is indeed continuing.

Responsibility for the implementation of the Anti-Dumping Agreement lies with the new Committee on Anti-Dumping Practices. This Committee is composed of representatives from each of the Members and will meet at least twice a year.

The DSB is the appropriate dispute body.

The view of *Kenneth Dam* at the time of the 1967 Anti-Dumping Code, that with all its detailed provisions, it was more a search for compromise solutions between the different trade practices of the various leading trading partners, than a targeted search to close off the existing loopholes and eliminate the weaknesses of the GATT anti-dumping regulation, would seem - even after the Uruguay Round - to still hold true (Dam, 1970: 174 f).

4.8 Agreement on Customs Valuation

The question of how a value is to be established for the purpose of customs valuation is a matter of considerable importance for international trade. GATT 47 did have a number of valuation principles, which as practice has shown, were inadequate to allow for a uniform approach to customs valuation on a world-wide basis. There were differences in all cases in which the actual invoice values were not ascertainable (for example, in-house deliveries, exchange of goods), where different customs duties systems operated, where older laws existed (in line with the principle "earlier law takes precedence"). It was with a view to eliminating these difficulties that an Agreement emerged from the Tokyo Round - Agreement on Implementation of Article VII of the GATT - which, largely unaltered, has been taken over by the WTO (Agreement on Implementation of Article VII of the General Agreement on Tariffs and Trade 1994).

The Agreement sets out five methods of establishing customs valuation as well as a catchall clause. The five methods are presented in the form of a hierarchy: if the customs valuation cannot be arrived at by using the first method, the second method will be used, and so on. The importer can seek to have recourse to methods four and five in reverse order.

First method: The customs value of the imported goods is the transaction value, that is, the price actually paid (including any commission and packing).

Second method: If the price actually paid cannot be determined, the customs value is the transaction value of identical goods which have been imported under the same competitive conditions. If no direct comparison is possible, an appropriate adjustment is allowed.

Third method: If neither of the first two methods is appropriate, the customs value will be the transaction value of similar (not like) products.

Fourth method: If none of the first three methods can be applied, it will be ascertained according to the selling price of the product in the country of importation, excluding the appropriate relevant costs and reasonable profit margin.

Fifth method: The customs value corresponds to the sum of the production costs, trade margin in the country of export as well as the related costs referred to in the first method above.

If the actual customs value of a product cannot be established by means of one of the five methods listed above, the customs authorities will determine the value, taking all relevant factors into account.

Non-industrial countries may delay application of the provisions of the Agreement for a period of five years.

In contrast to the 1981 Agreement, the new Agreement has no special provisions on dispute settlement. In the event of a dispute arising it should be referred to the DSB.

As regards the institutional aspects, there is a Committee on Customs Valuation, composed of representatives of each of the Members. This Committee meets once a year and is responsible for implementing the Agreement's provisions. A Technical Committee on Customs Valuation deals with matters of detail.

4.9 Agreement on Preshipment Inspection

The Agreement on Preshipment Inspection deals with export inspections carried out by private companies ("inspection entities") on behalf of government authorities. It is mainly the non-industrial countries which depend on private firms, because their own administrations are not in a position to allow them to deal adequately with capital outflows, means of circumventing export bans and customs fraud.

The Agreement requires the following to be observed when inspections are being conducted: non-discrimination between foreign trading partners (MFN); equal treatment between national and non-national importers and exporters; restriction of inspection to the customs territory of the Member; provision of information by all inspection entities of the inspection requirements to be fulfilled, including laws and regulations on which these are based; protection of confidential business information received in the course of the preshipment inspection, that is, no publication or passing on of information to third parties; avoiding unnecessary delays in carrying out the inspection; observing the mutually agreed inspection dates, as well as providing details of the inspection to those concerned within five working days.

Essentially, the inspection entities are to accept the contract price agreed between the importer and exporter unless the inspection entities establish exceptional price differences between the contract price and the price for identical, or similar goods, from the same country, at the same time and under the same conditions. Comparisons may not be made by reference to: selling price in the country of importation, prices of other countries of export, production costs, or price estimates.

The Agreement provides for the establishment of independent review entities to deal with disputes. These will be drawn from representatives of the inspection entities and an organization representing exporters of the country concerned. Disputes between the WTO Members are to be referred to the DSB.

4.10 Agreement on Rules of Origin

When GATT 47 refers to MFN and the equal treatment of domestic and imported products - as well as in its references to the regulation of quantitative restrictions - it uses terms such as "products from another country" or "products from the territory of another contracting party" without specifying exactly under what conditions or circumstances a good is to be regarded as originating in a country. It was in order to remove the ensuing lack of clarity that the Agreement now under consideration was drafted. This Agreement lays down that uniform rules of origin - applicable for all contracting parties - are to be drawn up within (the next) three years. This is the new hidden objective following previous efforts in this area. These previous efforts consisted of the attempts to achieve a world-wide harmonization in the area within the framework of the 1973 Kyoto Convention, which, being of a non-binding nature, only managed to achieve limited coverage.

The Agreement reached in the course of the Uruguay Round contains a number of basic principles for the three year transitional period as well as the follow-on definitive rules of origin. Existing autonomous non-preferential rules of origin are to be published and to be interpreted in conformity with the Agreement. The country of origin is to be determined in accordance with two criteria: in accordance with the criterion of where the product has been wholly obtained, or where the last substantial processing or transformation took place. Reference to the criterion of "last substantial processing or transformation" shows that even in the transitional period, the range of tariff headings within the tariff nomenclature is evident. In cases where the *ad valorem* percentage criterion is applied, the method for calculating this percentage is to be indicated, and in cases where the criterion of manufacturing or processing operation is prescribed, the manufacturing or processing operation conferring preferential origin is to be specified. Even during the transitional period, rules of origin may not be used as tools of trade policy, nor may they be used as trade barriers or discriminate against goods of foreign origin vis-à-vis domestic production. The Members must ensure a balanced, objective, unbiased administration of the rules of origin and are legally bound to provide information. The disputes procedure will ensure that administrative decisions can be processed further within the judicial process. Information is to be given within five months (and in the first year of the transitional period, as quickly as possible). Commercial and trade information is to be treated as confidential.

This Agreement assigns responsibility for the implementation of the technical annexes to the Committee on Rules of Origin - whose secretariat is provided by the WTO - and to the Technical Committee on Rules of Origin - reporting to the Customs Co-operation Council (CCC) in Brussels.

4.11 Agreement on Import Licensing Procedures

Import licences are no longer as important as they once were. Licensing is still a feature in trade in textiles and to some extent in trade in agriculture and primary products.

The main concern of the Agreement is to reduce the administrative demands connected with licensing to an absolute minimum and thus to reduce their restrictive effect on trade and to prevent discrimination between Members.

The Members are required to notify all details in respect of obtaining an import licence - application and expiry dates, existing exceptions as well as the number of licences to be granted. Information on the administrative procedures relating to the import licences must also be provided as must the intended division of the imports and - where available - the situation regarding imports as it now stands. In those cases where the licences are not expressly allocated to a particular country it will be at the discretion of the licence holder to choose the relevant country. In those instances where the licences are expressly connected to a particular country, the countries so advantaged, are to be made known. The Agreement requires that licence applications be processed within sixty days.

Members which institute licensing procedures are to advise the Committee of their rules (provision of product lists as well as contact points for information, administrative bodies for submission of applications and publication bodies). Domestic laws should conform to the provisions of the Agreement (by the time of the entry into force of the WTO Agreements).

The DSB will be the appropriate body for dealing with disputes between the Members.

4.12 Agreement on Subsidies and Countervailing Measures

Export subsidies and corresponding countervailing measures are of enormous importance in world trade and represent a critical element in the whole debate. The main recipients of subsidies in individual countries are unquestionably agriculture, mining, textiles, and ship-building.

At present, the provision of subsidies can be traced to two causes. In the first place the politicians and the authorities - particularly in times of recession - are put under pressure to address problems in the job market - both sectorally and regionally, to create jobs in the export field and to ensure that surplus production finds outlets on the world market. In addition, subsidies are seen as instruments of economic policy which are more flexible than changes in tariffs, or the introduction of quantitative restrictions or other protectionist measures.

The existing provisions dealing with subsidies were revised during the Uruguay Round and consolidated in the Agreement on Subsidies and Countervailing Measures. The Agreement defines a subsidy as a financial contribution by a government or any public body, in the form of a direct transfer of funds or other state measures, which promote exports or give an advantage to domestic goods over imports. The Agreement differentiates between specific and non-specific subsidies. Specific subsidies are directed at a defined industry or industries, or to an enterprise or group of enterprises excluding any third parties. Non-specific subsidies apply to all enterprises provided they fulfil certain conditions, which are known in advance. The central thrust of the Agreement is specific subsidies. Subsidies for agriculture are dealt with in the Agreement on Agriculture and do not fall within the framework of this Agreement.

The Agreement deals with three defined groups: subsidies which are automatically prohibited; subsidies which are prohibited to a degree; and subsidies which are allowed.

Prohibited subsidies include all those aids which, in law or in fact, together with other measures or by themselves, give an advantage to exports or to the use of domestic goods over imports. According to the Agreement these include: direct transfer of funds to companies in support of exports and similar practices equivalent to an export bonus; the preferential treatment of domestic exporters over foreign suppliers as regards lower transport and warehousing costs; state provision of cheap primary products to exporters; guaranteeing of advantages by means of direct or indirect tax system as well as in the calculation of social welfare costs, or the taking over by the state of export risks etc. The list of prohibited subsidies is not exhaustive. In the event of a Member suspecting that a fellow Member is providing prohibited export subsidies, the first party has the right to demand appropriate consultation. Should the negotiations not lead to a satisfactory outcome, all Members are entitled to lodge a formal complaint with the DSB. If the DSB and above all, the appeal hearing, determine that the complaint is well founded, the subsidies in question are to be withdrawn immediately, otherwise the injured country is entitled to introduce countervailing measures. The time limit for the DSB is three months and the Appellate Body has one month.

Subsidies which are prohibited to a certain degree are those which seriously injure, endanger or threaten the domestic industry of another country or which nullify or impair concessions and advantages stemming from the Agreement or which seriously prejudice the interests of another Member. According to the Agreement a serious injury or threat is suspected if the subsidies constitute more than 5 percent of the value of the product, if operating losses are covered by the state or, if monies owed to the state are written off, if demand for imports transfers to domestic production because of state aids, if in a particular market imports from a third country are displaced, impeded, etc. In all of these instances the Agreement transfers the burden of proof. The state granting the subsidies has to discharge the burden of proof and show that these state interventions have neither injured, nor threatened, the economy of another Member. Remaining differences are to be referred to the DSB.

Subsidies which are allowed include state intervention to support research and development in enterprises, research institutes and schools, regional aids as well as the payment of measures linked to the environment. Should a country show that it has been seriously prejudiced (injured or threatened) as a result of these subsidies (which are allowed) it is entitled to enter into negotiation and in the event of not being satisfied, is entitled to resort to countervailing measures.

The Agreement does say that in cases where the subsidies amount to less than one percent of the value of the product or where the injury is due to an oversight, the investigation should be curtailed. Furthermore, the Agreement lays down that the dispute settlement procedure normally should not last more than one year and in no instance should it take more than eighteen months. Countervailing measures adopted lapse after five years unless a fresh process is instituted.

Finally, the Agreement recognizes the possible importance of subsidies for non-industrial countries. Countries with an annual per capita income of less than US$ 1 000 are excluded from all subsidies provisions. For the remaining non-industrial countries (with an annual per capita income of more than US$ 1 000) the Agreement will only enter into force for these, and become legally binding, after a period of eight years.

4.13 Agreement on Safeguards

In the event that the obligations and concessions (for example, in the form of tariff concessions) arising from the WTO lead to a sudden increase in imports in the territory of one of the Members, or to a deterioration in import conditions which in turn represent a serious injury - or threat - to like or directly competitive domestic products, the Member is entitled to withdraw concessions granted - in total, or in part - or to amend them.

The Member in question should be consulted and given the opportunity to make the case - before the safeguard measures are applied. In critical circumstances, where delay would cause damage which it would be difficult to repair, a Member may take provisional safeguard measures. The duration of provisional measures may not exceed 200 days. An extension of these safeguard measures will depend on proper advance procedures. If the subsequent investigation indicates that the application of the provisional measures was not justified, the Member in question is then obliged to make good the losses.

No safeguard measures may be applied against a non-industrial country if its share of imports of the product in question is less than 3 percent, and the imports of such products from non-industrial countries in total, is less than 9 percent of these products.

The Members will notify the Committee on Safeguards when investigative processes are initiated or when safeguard measures are planned. The DSB will be the appropriate body for the Members in the event of a dispute.

5.   General Agreement on Trade in Services

The world trading system as covered by GATT 47 concentrated exclusively on trade in goods. Regulation of cross-border trade in services remained a matter for the individual countries. The non-inclusion of trade in services in the world trading system of the time can be traced to the then relative unimportance of international trade in services vis-à-vis its current position. Currently, international trade in services is approximately a fifth of the total trade in goods (although a precise separation between trade in goods and trade in services is not possible where services are built into the goods, such as is the case, for example, with computerized machines).

The 1986 Ministerial Conference requested that services be included in the world trading system then under discussion. It was intended that cross-border trade in services should also be subject to the most free and open markets.

At the beginning of the Uruguay Round it was primarily the industrial countries which were pushing for more open markets in the area of services. The non-industrial countries (under the leadership of Brazil and India) were opposed to this. This was partly due to fear of the growing competition to their own (state) service providers, and partly based on the argument that the proposals would pay scant attention to technology transfer, the international debt situation and international labour mobility. Towards the end of the negotiations a number of other areas of difficulty emerged - in maritime transport services, the audio-visual sector - these were in addition to the problems relating to the various positions of the non-industrialized countries (especially the financial services sector). The US was not prepared to accept substantial market access obligations in the maritime transport services sector. The European Communities - France in particular - were opposed to any liberalization in the audio-visual sector. The General Agreement on Trade in Services (GATS) which has emerged may be regarded as the lowest common denominator which it proved possible to agree on, but nonetheless, long-term, it does point in the direction of an open and free market.

The GATS has six parts, with a number of annexes each addressing one particular sector.

5.1 Definition of Service

The new world trading system is directed at the regulation of the international trade in services. Trade in services which is restricted to within national boundaries does not come within the scope of the Agreement.

The GATS distinguishes between four types of services.

1. The supply of services from country A to country B. Typical example of this would be planning carried out by an architect from country A for a client in country B (cross-border supply).

2. The supply of services in country A by the contemporaneous take up by a service recipient from country B. This would include primarily services in the tourism area (consumption abroad).

3. The supply of services by a provider of country A in country B by means of maintaining an agent or branch in country B (commercial presence).

4. The supply of services by a provider of country A in country B by means of the physical presence of a natural person in country B, possibly associated with the establishment of a business or residence in country B (presence of natural persons). Migrant workers seeking employment are excluded from the GATS.

If a country undertakes a market access commitment in relation to the supply of a service through the mode of supply referred to in numbers 1 and 3 above, this is automatically taken to include related transfers of capital (footnote 8 to GATS article XVI:1). GATS does not apply to those services which by means of value added are goods-related. These added values, such as goods-related insurance, banking, transport and warehousing services, come within the scope of the world trading system in goods, that is the GATT.

The GATS covers - according to article I:3 - all measures taken by all levels of the state, national government, as well as regional and local government, and authorities (such as federal, state, canton, municipality) as well as all non-governmental bodies which exercise powers delegated by any of the official levels outlined. The only exclusion relates to public service providers which are neither commercially run nor in competition with one or more service suppliers (exercising governmental authority) (see Senti, 1995: 3 ff).

5.2 Core Principle

The core principle of the GATS is - similar to the GATT - the MFN, found in part II. All advantages, favours, privileges and immunities which one Member accords to another country are to be accorded immediately and unconditionally for like services coming from another Member. In the event of changes to Schedules of concessions, due consideration is always to be given to the maintenance of MFN. Should a country withdraw a concession, an injured Member is entitled to compensation. The following areas do permit exemptions from MFN: (1) in the establishment of customs unions and free trade areas, if these free trade areas encompass almost all the trade of the countries involved and there is no negative effect on third parties: the same exemption has applied in cross-border trade in goods since the beginning of GATT, (2) in the creation of free trade areas in contiguous frontier zones in which the same services are produced and consumed, and (3) in all those areas which are indicated in the Agreement (for example telecommunications). The exemptions indicated enjoy a period of 10 years which, in case of necessity, can be extended.

As is the situation with the GATT, the GATS seeks to ensure that the principle of national treatment applies. This prevents a Member from according a provider of services, and services in total, less favourable treatment than that accorded domestic suppliers and services. For the present, however, national treatment in relation to services applies only to those services included in the Schedules.

The Agreement lays great emphasis on market transparency. The Members are obliged to publish all provisions and measures which affect cross-border trade in services. The Council for Trade in Services is to be notified of all provisions and measures. At the same time, the Members are to establish enquiry points to assist the other Members. Internal and confidential information of companies involved does not have to be published.

It is well known that the most important trade barriers in the services area are not to be found at the border, but exist rather in the form of domestic provisions (for example the requirement of a licence). The response of the Agreement to this is to require that Members apply such measures in a proportionate, objective and impartial manner.

In addition, the Members are asked to accord mutual recognition to educational qualifications including certificates and diplomas - whether directly, by means of harmonization, or by means of bilateral agreements with the trading partners. The Agreement permits the bilateral recognition, however, only on condition that negotiations will be entered into with other countries - at their request - on the question of recognition of examinations, certificates and diplomas. Mutual recognition may not lead to discrimination vis-à-vis other countries. The Council is to be notified of any bilateral agreements.

As with the GATT - which also allows measures to protect balance of payments - the GATS permits restrictions on grounds of balance of payments and currency reserves situations. The application of such measures should not discriminate between the Members, should not be inconsistent with IMF obligations, should not cause unnecessary economic damage to other countries, should not be excessive in the circumstances and should be of a temporary duration. The safeguards allowed date from the GATT of the 1940s and the period of fixed rates of exchange. Whether such exceptions are meaningful in a currency system with floating exchange rates remains an open question.

The safeguard measures in the GATS correspond to those in the GATT. Exceptions are allowed in relation to the protection of life and health of humans, animals, plants and the environment. Security exceptions are also allowed - within the same meaning.

5.3 Improved Market Access

In addition to addressing improved market access, the Agreement lists measures which are prohibited - in relation to international trade in services - in the absence of specific reservations in the Schedules. These prohibitions cover primarily: limitations on the number of service suppliers whether in the form of numerical quotas, monopolies, exclusive service suppliers or the requirements of an economic needs test; limitations on the total value of imported services by means of import quotas or economic needs test; limitations on the total number of natural persons (workers) who may be employed in a specific service sector; measures which restrict or require specific types of legal entity or joint ventures or the participation of capital or investment limits. The listing is not exhaustive but does serve to show the wide range of trade barriers which can apply in the services sector.

5.4 Institutional Measures

As indicated in section 2 above, there is a Council for Trade in Services and provision for the Council to set up corresponding working groups. The Council is entrusted with seeing that the Agreement and its contents are implemented.

Any differences which emerge between Members are to be tackled, in the first instance, by the parties entering into consultation with each other. Members may call on the Council or the DSB in respect of any matter for which it has not been possible to find a satisfactory solution through consultation. Excluded from this are the double taxation agreements between two or more countries. Differences in relation to double taxation agreements remain within the competence of the countries involved. A referral of tax matters to the Council or the DSB may be done only with the consent of both parties.

5.5 Supplementary Provisions

The Annexes to the GATS contain a number of supplementary provisions and exemptions essential to the Agreement. These emphasize the restricted effect of the overall treaty framework on services.

The first Annex refers to the movement of natural persons supplying services. Migrant worker policy, and thereby access to the labour market, are both subject to the GATS to the extent that a service activity is affected. In other words, as regards migrant worker policy, a country enjoys only so much freedom in this area as permitted by the absence of specific treaty commitments to the contrary.

A second Annex deals with the permitted exemptions in the financial sector. Every Member is entitled to adopt - and maintain - measures for the preservation of a healthy and stable financial market. The financial services referred to here would include primarily insurance services (for example, life and non-life insurances, reinsurance and retrocession, insurance intermediation such as brokerage and agency) and banking services (for example, lending of all types, including consumer credit, mortgage credit, guarantees and commitments, transferable securities, asset management). *Roland Wartenweiler* referred to an "apparent solution" in relation to the regulation of financial services: this is because in the fifth and sixth month after the entry into force of the WTO Agreement - over and beyond already established exceptions - every Member may improve, modify or withdraw all or part of the specific commitments included in its Schedule. This is at the discretion of the country concerned and without giving anything in return (see NZZ of 1.2.1994, No. 26: 33). Regulation of financial services, as it currently stands in the WTO system, clearly shows that in the closing stages of the negotiations, the USA was not prepared to accept the application of the MFN - as embedded in the framework Agreement - to the financial services sector. The United States has not (yet) signed the 1995 financial services agreement.

A third Annex to the GATS refers to the telecommunications sector. The objective is free access for Members to the telecommunication systems of the other Members, at appropriate cost level and under non-discriminatory conditions. The conditions attached to the use of the public telecommunication system should not be more stringent than is necessary for the proper maintenance of the system as regards organizational and technical matters. The Annex encourages the participants in a telecommunications system to engage in technical co-operation and to take particular account of the needs of the non-industrial countries. After the unsuccessful negotiations on telecommunications during the Uruguay Round, the WTO Ministers appointed a group of negotiators to continue the talks and conclude them before April 1996 at the latest. As no agreement was reached by the arranged date, the Members, approximately 50 at the time, decided to extend the deadline to 15 February 1997. On that date, the negotiating partners, whose number had in the meantime grown to 69, successfully concluded the negotiations.

The Agreement covers, according to the GATS Annexes, all measures of a Member which relate to entry to public telecommunication transport networks and services and their use. This includes telephone services, data transmission, telex, telegraph, fax, the use of private networks, cellular mobile telephone services, mobile data transmission and the Personal Communication System (PCS). Excluded from the negotiations were measures on cable or broadcast distribution of radio and television programmes, or on data processing. The negotiations concerned both the cross-border trade in services, as well as the deregulation within the WTO Members (commercial presence through agencies and branches). The Agreement reached foresees that a multilateral liberalization of the market in the area of telecommunication services will begin on 1 January 1998. The United States and the EU Member States will open their telecommunication markets relatively quickly and widely, with the exception of a few special regulations for certain Members, while other states like South Africa, Thailand, Trinidad and Tobago will not follow suit until the years 2000 to 2010. Greatly varying regulations still exist with regard to the issuing of licences and authorized capital participation.

The results of the telecommunication negotiations are to be extended in accordance with the Most-Favoured-Nation principle. In order to facilitate a successful conclusion to the negotiations, the Members were allowed to draw up MFN exemption lists.

Finally, the last Annex includes special provisions on air transport. According to this, the air transport agreements (bilateral and multilateral agreements on landing rights and other services which relate directly to air transport) are excluded from the GATS and from the uniform dispute settlement procedure. Not excluded are services which are confined to aircraft repair and maintenance services, the selling and marketing of air transport services and the computer reservation system (CRS) services. The Council for Trade in Services is encouraged to pay particular attention to the development of air transport with a view to further liberalization.

6. Agreement on Trade-Related Aspects of Intellectual Property Rights

The agreement on the protection of intellectual property rights in international trade (Agreement on Trade-Related Aspects of Intellectual Property Rights, TRIPS) represents the third pillar of the new world trading system - together with the GATT and the GATS. The TRIPS has two objectives: (1) co-ordination and integration of existing international provisions on the protection of intellectual property rights, and (2) adjustment and restructuring of applicable measures to the demands of an ever increasing interdependency in the field of international trade.

For a long time, international protection of intellectual property rights came within the remit of the Geneva based World Intellectual Property Organization (WIPO) - with its roots stretching back into the last century. The current situation is that the legal basis for the WIPO is the "Treaty on the Establishment of a World Intellectual Property Organization" signed in 1967, which entered into force in 1970. The WIPO is entrusted with the task of ensuring the world-wide protection of intellectual property rights by means of co-operation between the relevant national authorities. There are a number of international conventions which are of importance in this field: the 1883 Paris Convention for the Protection of Industrial Property - in its most recent version dating from 1979; the 1886 Berne Convention for the Protection of Literary and Artistic Works - in its most recent version dating from 1979, and the 1989 Treaty on Intellectual Property in Respect of Integrated Circuits (not yet in force). In addition to these, there are agreements on co-operation in protection of patents, trade marks, appellation of origin (geographical indications), utility models and industrial designs.

The Agreement (TRIPS) which emerged from the Uruguay Round is divided into seven parts. Part I deals with the WTO general principles (MFN, national treatment, market access, etc.), part II contains the obligations of the parties, part III deals with the enforcement and parts IV to VII deal with dispute prevention and settlement, special international (border protection) measures in the event of counterfeiting being suspected, transition arrangements as well as the institutional infrastructure.

6.1 General Principles

As already indicated in section 3.3, the general principles of the world trading system also apply to the protection of intellectual property rights and the national treatment of domestic and non-domestic holders of rights. MFN requires that all advantages, favours, privileges and immunities in relation to the protection of intellectual property rights granted by a Member to another country shall be accorded immediately and unconditionally to all other Members. Prior to this, the MFN principle had not appeared in this form in existing agreements and should therefore be regarded as an important innovation in relation to the protection of intellectual property rights.

National treatment of domestic and non-domestic owners of rights requires the Members, as regards the protection of intellectual property rights, to accord no less favourable treatment one to the other and to invoke no regulations which give an advantage to one over the other. This principle is incorporated in most of the existing agreements and therefore its inclusion in the TRIPS can be regarded as a confirmation of the existing situation.

Other general provisions of the Agreement refer to transparency in the administration, exchange of information and the recognition of the DSB.

Members are obliged to adopt national measures to protect national interests. These measures should not be contrary to the agreed WTO obligations. As a general rule, the Agreement sets out minimum requirements which the Members may exceed by introducing a higher level of protection - for example in the area of patents.

6.2 Individual Provisions

Part II regulates the individual areas of intellectual property rights and also extends these by the introduction of new areas, in particular the protection of commercial secrets.

The regulation of copyright and related rights corresponds to the Berne Convention on the Protection of Literary and Artistic Works. This has been extended by the TRIPS to include computer programmes and compilations of data - regardless of the form. An interesting extension of the TRIPS is the inclusion of rental rights. Authors of computer programmes and producers of phonograms (sound recordings) have the right to allow or to prohibit the commercial rental of their works. An exemption has been negotiated for Switzerland in that it can retain its system of purely compensation rights. The minimum term of protection for copyright is 50 years, whereas for broadcasting (wireless and television) the period is 20 years.

Owners of registered producers' brand and trademarks enjoy exclusive rights as regards usage by third parties. Third parties require the owner's consent in order to use the trademark in question. This applies equally to goods and to services. Trademarks should be registered for a term of no less than seven years. Renewal of registration is possible - indefinitely. If registration carries a use requirement, registration may be cancelled only after an uninterrupted period of at least three years of non-use.

Regarding geographical indications, Members are to ensure that these are not employed in a misleading or anti-competitive manner. Particular protection is provided for wine and other alcoholic drinks. Geographical indications should not be used for these goods, even when there is no real danger of confusion. Excluded from this are names which have achieved a generic status (such as Burgundy). The Agreement provides for continuing negotiation in relation to the geographical indications for wines.

Industrial designs are to be protected for a term of at least 10 years. The owner of a protected industrial design is entitled to prevent the use of his design by means of copies.

New patents enjoy a protection of 20 years. This applies for products, inventions and production processes in all fields of technology. Excluded from patentability are inventions whose exploitation is prohibited on grounds of *ordre public* or morality. Permissible exclusions include plants and animals but not, however, micro-organisms.

In the area of integrated circuits, the TRIPS anticipates adherence to the 1989 Agreement - opened for signature in May 1989 in Washington (Treaty on Intellectual Property in Respect of Integrated Circuits). There is a minimum term of protection of 10 years as an extension to this Agreement.

Finally, the TRIPS requires that data and commercial secrets - submitted to governments or governmental agencies in the course of seeking approval - be protected.

6.3 Legal Enforcement

Part III of the TRIPS requires the Members to ensure that the obligations undertaken are fulfilled without regard to the nationality of the parties to the proceedings, unreasonable time-limits, disproportionately complicated bureaucracy or costs.

The judicial authorities may resort to injunctions in the event that delays might lead to irreparable harm. Customs authorities may withhold suspicious counterfeit goods and suspected pirated goods at the border for a reasonable period of time, in order to prevent the release into free circulation of such goods. Criminal procedures and penalties will be applied in the event of a breach.

The transitional periods in the Agreement are one year for the industrial countries, five years for the non-industrial countries and those countries in the process of changing from a centrally planned economy to a market economy, and eleven years for the least-developed countries - although these can benefit from practically limitless exceptions. The provision on non-discrimination applies from the date of entry into force of the Agreement: there is no transitional period applicable.

Disputes between the Members are to be referred to the DSB unless exception provisions apply.

6.4 Institutional Provisions and Exceptions

The Council for TRIPS monitors the operation of the Agreement. It is also responsible for cooperation with other international organizations (for example, the WIPO) as well as providing legal advice for the Members.

The TRIPS Council will review the Agreement after the expiration of the transitional period of five years. In so doing, it will take the experience gained into account. Shorter time limits apply in relation to the patentability of living organisms. Other reviews will take place every two years.

The Agreement calls on the Members to establish information points within the national administration, and to provide for the mutual granting of legal assistance.

As with the GATT, the TRIPS has security exceptions. Each Member is free to withhold information on the grounds of security and to take any action in relation to the nuclear industry or arms industry - without taking account of the TRIPS.

7. The Plurilateral Agreements

In sections 4, 5 and 6 we dealt with those agreements which are binding on all contracting parties, that is, the multilateral agreements. The multilateral agreements include the GATT, the GATS and the TRIPS, together with the special agreements on agriculture, anti-dumping, subsidies, etc.

In addition to the multilateral agreements four other agreements were annexed to the WTO - binding only on those countries which agreed to be bound by them. In contrast to the multilateral agreements, these are plurilateral agreements. These include the Agreement on Trade in Civil Aircraft, the Agreement on Government Procurement, the International Dairy Agreement and the International Bovine Meat Agreement. These agreements date from the Tokyo Round and with the exception of the Agreement on Government Procurement, have been subsumed into the WTO system practically unchanged. The Agreement on Government Procurement has been brought into line with the other WTO Agreements, widened as far as the sub-national level is concerned and deepened as regards the Schedules (of concessions).

"Whereas multilateral agreements guarantee the world-wide uniformity of the conventional structure" said *Roland Wartenweiler* "plurilateral agreements lead to a legal system of variable geometry. This heterogeneity of international trading rules is not completely without danger and could undermine the entire system if not handled carefully. That this state of affairs is recognized is to be seen from the fact that in the WTO, as far as the current world trading system is concerned, plurilateralism has clearly been reined in to the benefit of a real multilateralism" (NZZ of 15.3.1994, No. 62:35 translated).

In September 1997 it was decided to delete the Agreements on Meat and Dairy Products from the WTO. The reasons advanced were "in the interest of economy and efficiency" as well as "the resource constraints faced by governments [and] the Secretariat". These two Agreements are terminated as of end of 1997.

7.1 Agreement on Trade in Civil Aircraft

During the Tokyo Round a number of countries (Canada, Japan, Sweden, the USA and the European Communities) took the opportunity, within the framework of the GATT negotiations, to address the question of competition in relation to trade in civil aircraft. The Agreement which emerged from these negotiations (Agreement on Trade in Civil Aircraft) entered into force on 1 January 1980. According to the latest Activity Report (BISD, 40 s/518 et seq.) there are currently twenty-three Signatories - mainly from Europe and North America as well as Japan.

The objective of the Agreement is to establish a trade régime which is as liberal as possible, dealing with civil aircraft, engines and parts as well as flight simulators and their components. There is a detailed listing of the products which come within the scope of the Agreement in an Annex (to the Agreement). The creation of uniform conditions dealing with competition should reduce the negative impact of state intervention to a minimum. Government procurement is subject to commercial criteria - such as price, quality, delivery times. All Signatories to the Agreement enjoy the same right of access to tendering - under the same conditions as all other countries. The Agreement on Subsidies and Countervailing Measures applies to trade in civil aircraft.

As indicated in its title, the Agreement covers trade in civil aircraft only. Procurement of military aircraft and parts for non-civilian usage are expressly excluded.

The Agreement requires that any disputes which arise are to be addressed through consultation and by concerted action to find a solution. If no settlement can be reached, the DSB may be called on.

In 1992 the Committee decided on a revision of the Agreement and to seek a broader membership. The outcome of ongoing negotiations seems to indicate the possible integration of the bilateral agreement between the USA and the European Communities into the WTO. There are no further indications of progress at the time of writing (Summer, 1997).

7.2 Agreement on Government Procurement

International trade differentiates between state imports in the following way:

- those destined for resale or for the manufacture of products for resale

- those purchased for the state's own use - that is, not destined for commercial purposes

If a state enters the international market either as a trader or manufacturer - that is as a vendor or purchaser - it is then obliged, as a GATT contracting party, to observe the general principle of non-discrimination "prescribed in this Agreement (GATT) for governmental measures affecting imports or exports by private traders" (GATT, article XVII:1a). This form of activity is described as "state-trading" in the parlance of international trade.

On the other hand, if the state is the ultimate consumer of the imported products, it is absolved from the requirement to observe GATT obligation of non-discrimination and national treatment. What GATT then requires is that there is "fair and equitable treatment" accorded to the trade of the other contracting parties (GATT, article XVII:2). Purchases made by the state where it is the ultimate consumer are known as "government procurement".

During the drafting period of the ITO in the 1940s there was an attempt by some countries to have government procurement - as opposed to actual state trading - excluded from the obligations of non-discrimination and national treatment. They were not prepared to give up their freedoms in this area. GATT 47 took over the principles set out in the Havana Charter with only some minor editorial amendments.

During the 1940s and 1950s government procurement in the industrial countries amounted to between 10 percent and 15 percent of GDP. In the 1970s and 1980s this rose to between 20 percent and 40 percent. It was as a result of the increasing importance of this area that the contracting parties addressed the issue during the course of the Tokyo Round. Negotiations were concluded on this Agreement in April 1979 and it entered into force on 1 January 1981. Some aspects of the Agreement were revised during the Uruguay Round and were signed - as were the rest of the Agreements - in Marrakesh on 15 April 1994. The Agreement entered into force on ratification by the Parties. The current Parties are Canada, the European Communities, Israel, Japan, Korea, Norway, Switzerland and the USA. Only Hong Kong - currently a Party - has not signed the new Agreement. Thirty-five governments enjoy observer status.

Objective and Scope

The Agreement has two main objectives: (1) Equal treatment of domestic and foreign suppliers and goods within the framework of the Agreement (national treatment) and (2) non-discrimination regarding the suppliers and goods between Parties to the Agreement (MFN).

These two principles (national treatment and MFN) may not be circumvented by recourse to technical specifications. This obligation is addressed by the application of the Agreement on Technical Barriers to Trade to government procurement.

The current Agreement addresses:

- all laws, regulations, procedures and practices observed by public authorities (of those Parties to the Agreement) in relation to government procurement in the area of products and services. The extension of the Agreement to include services is one of the results of the Uruguay Round.

- the governments and authorities of the Parties as well as the numerous sub-national bodies such as states or cantons (in federal states), municipal authorities (including councils) and public bodies (including corporations) - these sub-national bodies being a recent innovation. As an example - taking the Swiss context - the first Annex to the Agreement mentions the Eidgenoessische Drucksachen- und Materialzentrale, the Landesbibliothek, the Bundesbauamt, the Technischen Hochschulen in Zurich and Lausanne. The second Annex lists all the cantons, and the third Annex covers individual enterprises at municipal level and public bodies such as the Wasserverbund Regio Berne, the Nordostschweizerischen Kraftwerke AG, the Swiss Post, Telephone and Telegraph company (PTT), the Verkehrsbetriebe Zurich and Zurich-Kloten airport.

- contracts of a certain monetary value. The new Agreement sets down certain monetary values (which are to be regarded as trigger values) for government procurement of products, services and construction at national and sub-national level. At the national level, the trigger value for products and services is 130 000 SDR (ca US$ 180 000), at the sub-national level (provinces, states and cantons) the relevant value is 200 000 SDR and the trigger value for state enterprises and public bodies is 400 000 SDR. The Parties agreed on a figure of 5 million SDR for construction works. There are some differences in trigger values for Canada, Israel and the USA (higher values for products and services for the sub-national level in Canada and the USA, higher value in relation to construction work for Israel). The Annexes list the relevant state enterprises and public bodies.

Procedure for Awarding Contracts

The Agreement refers to current accepted practices: open, selective and invitation to tender procedures. An open procedure allows for all interested suppliers to submit a tender. In cases where a selective procedure is used, tenders are received only from those (potential) suppliers who are invited to tender. Finally, in cases of invitation to tender, the purchaser contacts suppliers individually (in cases where the other two procedures are regarded as unsuitable).

In the open and selective procedures the purchaser makes an initial qualitative selection in what is called the qualification procedure. In order to make an actual selection it is necessary to make available - in advance - all necessary requirements to be met. Publication of the requirements should include: type and quantity of the goods, type of procedure, delivery point, place of application, technical and financial requirements as well as payment methods. Place of publication is to be chosen from those listed in the Agreement. Where the selective procedure is used the purchasing bodies must publish - annually - a list of the qualified suppliers, including the conditions for admission to these lists, as well as an enumeration of the products purchased in accordance with this procedure.

The Agreement sets down that application deadlines and delivery times should be in line with normal commercial practices. Application forms and details sent to suppliers should be complete and sufficient to allow for a proper tender (administrative and technical matters).

Tenders are to be received, held and opened in a properly constituted manner. The opening of the tenders should take place in the presence of the parties tendering, or their representatives, or of impartial observers. As far as this aspect of the procedure is concerned, the Agreement emphasizes that the acceptance and opening of the tenders "should reflect the provisions of this Agreement on national treatment and non-discrimination".

Tenders can be invited if either of the alternatives does not result in sufficient interest being shown, if the subject matter is a work of art for which there is no "reasonable alternative", for reasons of utmost urgency, in relation to additional services, if a prototype is being made or in the case of an original manufacture. Invitation to tender should not be followed with a view to preventing the greatest possible competition; likewise, it should not be used to protect domestic producers or to discriminate between foreign suppliers.

The Agreement does not lay down any specific criteria for awarding the contract. Whoever is awarding the contract is free to decide on, and take into account, additional factors to the price such as quality, service, delivery times, spare parts availability etc. The additional factors are to be made known in advance. The Parties are to refrain from imposing, seeking or considering offsets in the qualification and selection of suppliers, products, services, or in the valuation of tenders and award of contracts.

As regards exception clauses, the Agreement draws largely on articles XX and XXI of GATT.

The Agreement requires that no provisions should be so interpreted that the Parties are prevented from deciding on, or carrying through, measures for the protection of public morality, order, security, the protection of life and health of humans, animals or plants, protection of intellectual property or in relation to the disabled, charitable institutions or goods manufactured in prisons.

Furthermore, article XXIII of the Agreement may not prevent the Parties "adopting measures or refusing information for the protection of their essential security interests in connection with the manufacture of weapons, munitions or materials of war or indispensable procurement in relation to national security or national defence in so far as these are regarded as necessary".

Non-industrial countries

The Parties are requested to take particular account of the situation in the non-industrial countries. This should manifest itself in a number of different ways. It should find expression in the setting up of information centres in the industrial countries in order to facilitate market access for the non-industrial countries. It should also manifest itself in the granting of all necessary technical assistance to the non-industrial countries in connection with government procurement.

The Parties are authorized to conclude unilateral treaties with the non-industrial countries in order to guarantee advantages which are not to be passed on to the other countries. Individual countries and groups of countries have already concluded such treaties (for example, the European Communities within the framework of the Lomé Agreement).

7.3 International Dairy Agreement

The International Dairy Agreement was a response to the unsuccessful outcome of the Tokyo Round in so far as agriculture was concerned. This was similar to the situation with the Bovine Meat Agreement (see 7.4). The Dairy Agreement entered into force on 1 January 1980 and has been extended every three years since then. The extensions followed automatically provided that the participants did not put forward any alternative demands. Originally, the key point for discussion was the maximum price for international trade in dairy products. The importing countries did not show any enthusiasm for this and the exporting countries were opposed to it. The prices then in discussion were at a level which was unattractive for the industrial countries. Quite in contrast to the original thinking of the negotiating delegations, the participants finally settled on an agreement laying down minimum prices for specific export products as well as detailed provisions on the mutual information and consultation obligations of the participants. The Agreement expired on 31 December 1994 and then became part of the WTO framework.

Participants

In November 1984, as a result of pressure from the then European Communities, the Butter Protocol annexed to the Agreement was suspended in order to allow for the EEC cheap butter export activities. The USA and Austria (not then a Member State of the EU) withdrew from the Agreement in protest. The current participants are Argentina, Australia, Bulgaria, the European Communities, Egypt, Hungary, Japan, New Zealand, Norway, Poland, Romania, Switzerland, South Africa and Uruguay. Major trading partners such as the USA either do not take part in the Agreement or, as with the EC for example, use it at will. As far as smaller countries are concerned, the Agreement is irrelevant both as regards pricing and quantities either because they do not export dairy products (such as Romania or Uruguay for example) or because the price level is such that it is considerably more than the minimum price.

Contents

In its current form the International Dairy Agreement is a sectoral price cartel, negotiated and arrived at, within the framework of GATT and as such, contradicts both the letter and the spirit of the goals of the GATT and the WTO - the objectives of which are a free and open world trading system. The countries exporting dairy products (skimmed milk, milk powder, butter milk powder, milk fat and cheese) are obliged, according to the Agreement, not to export below a certain minimum price, while the importing countries are expected to cooperate in the realization of these minimum prices. The minimum prices set out in the Agreement may be amended by the Committee taking into account "the results of the operation of the Protocol on the one hand, and the development of the international market on the other".

In contrast to the laying down of the minimum price, the obligation on each side to provide information reflects the WTO objective of increased market transparency. The participants are obliged to inform the Council "at regular intervals and within the shortest possible time" of details which it requires for monitoring and analyzing the situation on the world market for each individual dairy product. This information relates to the production, the storage, the prices, as well as the import and export of the relevant products; in addition, it includes information on existing or anticipated trade measures and bilateral, plurilateral or multilateral obligations in the area of dairy products.

Particular attention to the situation in the non-industrial countries was required and the industrial countries asked to view all requests for technical assistance in a positive fashion.

The Agreement also addresses the question of food aid. The participants are asked, independently, within the limits of what is feasible for them, to supply dairy products to the non-industrial countries and to improve coordination of these efforts.

Institutional Provisions

The International Council for Dairy Products was given the task i.a. of collecting and analyzing the market information. A committee was established for each of the product groups - milk powder, milk fat and cheese - each with the task of preparing a market report on its product area. These reports have been published annually (GATT, The World Market for Dairy Products).

1998 onwards

In September 1997 the International Dairy Council agreed to terminate the Agreement at the end of 1997. The provision of regular market information on Dairy Products will now be done by national and intergovernmental bodies.

7.4 International Bovine Meat Agreement

This Agreement was a response to the unresolved difficulties in the agricultural area - similar to the situation with the International Dairy Agreement. The Agreement, which entered into force on 1 January 1980, arose from the fact that agriculture was not dealt with during the Tokyo Round. The Agreement was based on the belief that active intensive cooperation between the trading partners would lead to the liberalization and stability of international trade in live animals and meat. The Agreement was extended at the beginning of 1992 to run until the end of 1994. It will terminate at the end of 1997. At the last count there were twenty-seven participants with forty-one countries (EC representing the fifteen EU Member States). The countries concerned represent the main players in the area, either as importers or exporters of bovine meat (meat and live animals): the countries of North America and Europe, Argentina, Brazil, Colombia, Paraguay and Uruguay from Latin America, Egypt, Nigeria, Tunisia, South Africa from the African continent, Australia, New Zealand and Japan.

Contents

The Agreement deals exclusively with live animals and bovine meat, fresh, chilled, frozen, dried or smoked. In contrast to the Dairy Agreement there are no provisions on minimum or maximum prices. The thrust is exclusively mutual exchange of information and monitoring of the market. The participants were obliged to notify the Council of data on production, stocks, prices, trade quantities, marketing measures and agreements with other countries. This information was to enable the Council to monitor the world bovine meat market and to arrive at appropriate decisions. If as a result of this market analysis, the Council noted that there is a serious im- balance in the world meat market it would endeavour - taking the situation in the non-industrial countries into account and seeking consensus by means of examination by the governments - to indicate possible remedial measures (art. IV:2).

Following the same formulation as in the Dairy Agreement, the indus- trial countries were requested to take the situation in the non-industrial countries into consideration and to respond positively to requests for technical assistance.

Institutional Provisions

The Agreement provided for the setting up of an International Meat Council, with representatives of the participating countries. Meetings of the Council were scheduled to take place at least twice a year, to deliberate on the state of the world market. From what can be gleaned in recent years it would seem that the participating countries are slow to fulfil their obligations as regards providing information.

1998 onwards

As has already been indicated, this Agreement will terminate at the end of 1997. The parties will now rely on information prepared regularly by national and intergovernmental bodies.

Outlook

On 15 September 1986 *Julio Maria Sanguinetti,* President of Uruguay, opened the eighth round of trade talks within the framework of the GATT, in Punta del Este, with these words of warning: "we have to decide whether we are going to promote active and vigorous trade with equal opportunities for all, or whether we will choose the path of trade wars" (GATT, FOCUS, 1986/41:7). Seven years later, *Peter Sutherland,* Director-General of the GATT, closed the round with a thought-provoking comment: "Today the world has chosen openness and co-operation instead of uncertainty and conflict" (GATT, FOCUS, 1993/104:1). The black and white metaphors employed by the diplomats involved in the negotiations in relation to the success or failure of the negotiations should not be understood as clear indication that, had the Uruguay Round failed, this would have led to chaos in world trade. Equally it should be understood that success does not mean that all problems with world trade have been solved. The results which have emerged from the seven years of negotiations are in many instances compromises, what was possible in the circumstances, a common denominator, but - and this is essential - directed at political stability, raising the standard of living, full employment, production which enhances the environment and co-operation between industrial and non-industrial countries. These goals will never be completely achieved but they do point the way forward in the fashioning of national and international trade policies.

Satisfactory implementation of the results of the Uruguay Round negotiations required, in the first instance, that the treaties be ratified by an appropriate number of countries reflecting a good geographical distribution. The treaties entered into force on 1 January 1995. Some provisions were applicable immediately on the entry into force - for example the new dispute settlement procedure, the anti-dumping and subsidies provisions as well as the sanitary and phytosanitary requirements. The reduction of tariffs is to follow in prescribed periods over five years after the entry into force of the WTO. Six years are envisaged for market access and removal of trade barriers in agriculture. Transitional periods of up to ten years are included in the Textiles and Clothing Agreement. In general, non-industrial countries enjoy longer transitional periods than industrial countries.

Adjustments within the individual WTO Members' countries are also necessary. For example, the new world trading system requires that the agricultural policy of certain countries be restructured; non-tariff barriers are to be converted into tariffs (tariffication) and product-related income supports replaced with product-based direct payments. It is quite obvious that such changes in the system will lead to battles to protect ground held.

Many problem areas could not be settled during the Uruguay Round: how is the danger posed by regionalism to be dealt with in a system which strives for global market access? Is it not the case that the strengthened free trade areas and customs unions represent a latent threat to the WTO? Will it be possible to bring about labour mobility within the cross-border movement of services? Under what conditions can financial services and the audio-visual area be integrated into the existing Agreement on services? How is the environment to be tackled in the framework of open international trade? What strategy is to be employed in relation to the non-industrial countries? No doubt these, and similar such questions, will form part of the next round of negotiations.

Whatever the shortcomings and inadequacies of the results of the Uruguay Round, the new Agreement is a logical progression of what had already been achieved within the framework of the General Agreement on Tariffs and Trade (GATT) - a partial success in the inclusion of new trade areas such as services and the protection of intellectual property rights, as well as a long-term objective for the foreign trade policy strategies of the WTO Members.

Bibliography and further reading

Baldwin, Robert E. (1993), Adapting the GATT to a more regionalized world: a political economy perspective, in: Anderson, K. and Blackhurst, R. (Eds.), Regional Integration and the Global Trading System, New York etc., pp 387-407

Baldwin, Robert E. (1970), Nontariff Distortions of International Trade, Washington, D.C.

Benedek, Wolfgang (1990), Die Rechtsordnung des GATT aus völkerrechtlicher Sicht, Berlin etc.

Beise, Marc (1993), Freihandel und Umwelt, Ein GATT-Thema der 90er Jahre, Unterlage zur Tagung der International Law Association (ILA) - German Branch, Tuebingen

Beise, Marc (1994), Vom alten zum neuen GATT - Zu den neuen Dimensionen der Welthandelsordnung, in: Vitzthum, W. G. (Ed.), Europaeische und internationale Wirtschaftsordnung aus der Sicht der Bundesrepublik Deutschland, Baden-Baden, pp 179-224

Cottier, Thomas (1992), Intellectual Property in International Trade Law and Policy: The GATT Connection, in: Aussenwirtschaft, Volume 47, Issue I, pp 79-105

Dam, Kenneth W. (1970), The GATT, Law and International Economic Organization, Chicago and London

Deutsches Institut fuer Wirtschaftsforschung (DIW), Uruguay-Runde und Dienstleistungshandel, Wochenbericht 34/93, pp 467-470

Diem, Andreas (1996), Freihandel und Umweltschutz, Baden-Baden

GATT, Activities (annually)

GATT, Basic Instruments and Selected Documents BISD, (annually)

GATT, International Trade (annually)

GATT, News of the Uruguay Round

GATT, Newsletter, FOCUS (monthly)

GATT (1994), Final Act Embodying the Results of the Uruguay Round of Multilateral Trade Negotiations, UR-94-0083, Marrakesh, 15 April 1994

GATT (1958), Trends in International Trade, Geneva (Haberler Report)

Hallstroem, Paer (1994), The GATT Panels and the Formation of International Trade Law, Stockholm

Hudec, Robert E. (1993), GATT Dispute Settlement, in: Minnesota Journal of Global Trade, Volume 2, Issue 1, pp 1-113

Hummer, Waldemar und Weiss, Friedl, Vom GATT'47 zum WTO'94 (Collection of all treaty texts), Baden-Baden, Zurich and Vienna

ifo Institut fuer Wirtschaftsforschung, "ifo Schnelldienst" Munich (3 times/month)

Jackson, John H. (1989), Restructuring the GATT System, London

Jackson, John H. (1969), World Trade and the Law of GATT, Indianapolis etc.

Kock, Karin (1969), International Trade Policy and the GATT 1947-1967, Stockholm

Langhammer, Rolf J. (1994), Nach dem Ende der Uruguay-Runde: Das GATT am Ende? Kieler Diskussionsbeitraege, No. 228, Institut fuer Weltwirtschaft, Kiel

Oppermann, Thomas, and Baumann, Jutta (1993), Handelsbezogener Schutz geistigen Eigentums, in ORDO, Jahrbuch fuer die Ordnung von Wirtschaft und Gesellschaft, Volume 44, pp 121-137

Petersmann, Ernst-Ulrich (1997), The GATT/WTO Dispute Settlement System, London etc.

Petersmann, Ernst-Ulrich (1993), International Trade Law and International Environmental Law, in: Journal of World Trade, Volume 27, No. 1, pp 43-81

Roessler, Frieder (1993), The relationship between regional integration agreements and the multilateral trade order, in: Anderson, K. and Blackhurst, R. (Eds.), Regional Integration and the Global Trading System, New York etc., pp 311-325

Schuknecht, Ludger (1992), Trade Protection in the European Community, Chur etc.

Senti, Richard (1995), Das Dienstleistungsabkommen im Rahmen der WTO, in: LJZ, Liechtensteinische Juristenzeitung, Volume 16, Issue 3, pp 3-11

Senti, Richard (1986), GATT, System der Welthandelsordnung, Zuerich

Senti, Richard (1994a), GATT-WTO, Die neue Welthandelsordnung nach der Uruguay Runde, Zürich

Senti, Richard (1994b), Die Integration als Gefahr fuer das GATT, in: Aussenwirtschaft, Volume 49, Issue 1, pp 131-150

Wartenweiler, R., Gemperle, R., u.a. (1994), Vom GATT zur WTO, Series of articles in NZZ, Nos. 18, 20, 26, 32, 38, 44, 50, 62, 68 and 74

WTO, Annual Report

WTO, Newsletter, FOCUS (monthly)

Index

Major page references are in bold. References followed by t refer to tables.

Index

Index

Index